S0-BFD-174

"NICE GIRLS DON'T GET RAPED"

"NICE GIRLS DON'T GET RAPED"

Jennifer Botkin-Maher

 Here's Life Publishers

Published by
HERE'S LIFE PUBLISHERS, INC.
P.O. Box 1576
San Bernardino, CA 92402

HLP Product Number 951624
©1987, Jennifer Botkin-Maher
All rights reserved.
Printed in the United States of America

Library of Congress Cataloging-in-Publication Data

Botkin-Maher, Jennifer, 1945-
　"Nice girls don't get raped."
　　1. Botkin-Maher, Jennifer, 1945-　　. 2. Rape
victims — United States — Biography.　3. Rape — United States.
4. Rape victims — Services for — United States.
I. Title
HV6561.B67　1987　　　362.8'8　　　　86-22770
ISBN 0-89840-157-7 (pbk.)

Unless otherwise indicated, Scripture quotations are from the *New American Standard Bible,* © The Lockman Foundation 1960, 1962, 1963, 1968, 1971, 1972, 1975, 1977, and are used by permission.

FOR MORE INFORMATION, WRITE:

L.I.F.E. — P.O. Box A399, Sydney South 2000, Australia
Campus Crusade for Christ of Canada — Box 300, Vancouver, B.C. V6C 2X3, Canada
Campus Crusade for Christ — 103 Friar Street, Reading RG1 1EP, Berkshire, England
Lay Institute for Evangelism — P.O. Box 8786, Auckland 3, New Zealand
Great Commission Movement of Nigeria — P.O. Box 500, Jos, Plateau State Nigeria, West Africa
Campus Crusade for Christ International — Arrowhead Springs, San Bernardino, CA 92414, U.S.A.

Dedicated to each of you who have experienced the nightmare of rape. May you find renewed strength and hope for recovery, and be challenged to press on.

CONTENTS

ACKNOWLEDGMENTS

Helen Wessel who watered the seed planted by the Holy Spirit.

Jo Berry who challenged me to succeed.

Jody Groves who dried my tears.

Lois Lingard who accepted me without asking questions.

Tony Legrand who gave sacrificial support.

John P. Epp, pastor, who said, "If you'll trust God, He can use this setback as a stepping stone."

Cheryl Sansone whose faithful friendship of seventeen years continues to validate my blossoming.

Norm and Virginia Rohrer who consistently encouraged me to press on.

Fritz Ridenour who exhorted me to go back and begin again — this time with honest expression of my pain.

Patty Christiansen who sustained me through prayer during months of writing and rewriting.

Neva B. True who gave me retreat at her mountain cabin to complete my manuscript, and who prepared all the meals.

Bev Hamilton who praised my efforts to continue after receiving twenty rejections.

Kathy Collard Miller who always believed in me.

Leslie H. Stobbe, president, Here's Life Publishers, who gave me this opportunity to impact others for Christ as a professional writer.

Jean Bryant, my editor, whose patience, skill and expert editorial eye gave focus to my ramblings.

Nick Maher, my husband, who inspired my courage in gaining triumph over tragedy.

Nicole Maher, seventeen, who was proud of me and surprised me with love notes at my desk.

Lisa Maher, sixteen, who frequently made dinner and brought me coffee late at night when I was working.

Amy Maher, eleven, who rubbed my tired shoulders and said, "Mom, your book's *going* to get published!"

My extended family who all loved and affirmed me during the long years of work and research.

The many unmentioned friends and colleagues who undergirded and guided me in my insecurities — a special thank you. And finally, my Grannie who once said, "Always remember, Grannie loves ya."

1

Shadow of Death

It's a beautiful, "God's in His heaven, all's right with the world," picture-postcard-perfect California day. Amy, my two-year-old, is napping. Nicole and Lisa are at school. Nick, my husband, left just twenty minutes ago to play golf and won't be home until dinnertime, about 6 P.M. In essence, I'm alone. I decide to putter in the back yard, bask in the warmth of the sun, and repot some plants. Halfway through my task, I need more pots.

I go into my kitchen and am rummaging through the cupboards, looking for containers, when I feel a tap on my shoulder. It is so faint that I think my imagination is playing tricks on me. The house is quiet except for the sound of the pans I'm rattling during my search. I haven't heard the doorbell ring or anyone knock.

A second tap on my shoulder jolts me back to reality. I turn, half expecting to see Nick, thinking he must have forgotten some clubs he needed for his golf game. I am not prepared to face some grotesque stranger who is masquerading as a pumpkin, his head covered with a faded orange hood; his eyes, nose and mouth gaping at me through roughly cut holes. The jagged bottom of his mask rests on his broad,

11

unclothed shoulders. Bulging muscles pull the flesh taut on
his upper arms. His olive-skinned chest is hairless; his feet bare.

Horrified by this bizarre-looking creature, I bolt upright
and scream uncontrollably. *Surely someone will hear me.
Someone will come! Someone! No wonder I didn't hear any
footsteps. He doesn't have on shoes. He must have followed
me in from the back yard. Dear Lord, why didn't I close the
door when I came in? He's holding something in his hand.
What is it?* It glistens in the sunlight. *Dear God, it's a knife!*

"Stop screaming," he orders in a steady voice.

I abruptly comply, terrified of the consequences of dis-
obedience. He eases the sharp edge of the blade toward my
shoulder. I fall back against the counter, clutching the rim for
support. *Have my screams wakened Amy? Is she still asleep?
If she is awake, will she call out for me as she always does?
Oh, dear Lord, keep her asleep.*

He grabs my upper arm. My eyes widen, my mouth is
dry, my chilled body shakes despite the heat of the day. *Who
is he? Where did he come from? What does he want? I know!
This must be some sort of sick joke. Yes, that's it. Somebody
is playing a joke on me, trying to scare me. Any minute now
he'll take off that hideous hood and collapse laughing, his
perverted sense of humor satisfied.*

*Or, maybe he's here to rob us. In that case, the joke's
on him. Will he believe me when I tell him we don't have
any valuables? Or will that make him mad, and will he use
that knife on me?*

Finally, I think the unthinkable. *He is not here to rob
us. He is going to rape me. No! Oh, God, no! If I don't
think about it, maybe he'll go away. This can't be happening.
Nice girls don't get raped!*

He tightens his grip. My arm aches. No more wondering.
This wild man means business. I try to appear naive, hoping
that acting innocent will make him want to go. *A man like
this would want an experienced woman, wouldn't he?*

"What do you want?" I barely whisper, surprised that I
can speak at all — my vocal chords feel paralyzed by fear.

"I want you," he says in an unfaltering, firm, cold voice.

I am immobilized by sheer terror. For the first time in

my life I understand how someone can literally be frightened to death. I wonder if it might happen to me. Frozen, unable to move or think clearly, I pray. *God, help me. I haven't done anything wrong. Please, God, make him leave. I am so scared.*

What am I going to do? I must think! I must plan! I mustn't let him see how frightened I am, how helpless and impotent I feel. Can he see through me? Does he know I'm terrified? Nick, I desperately need you. Please come home. Why, oh why didn't I come in earlier when I felt I was being watched? If he just didn't have that knife, maybe somehow I could fight him off and get away. Should I try? I don't know if I'm strong enough. What if I fail and get stabbed in a struggle? Amy! I can't try to escape and leave her in the house with this madman. I am trapped, totally at the mercy of a maniac.

"Who's here?" he blares.

"Uh . . . well . . . uh. . . ." The words won't come. *Should I say that my husband is in the other room, or did he watch Nick leave? What will he do to me if I lie? If I lie, he'll find out anyway.*

"My daughter is asleep in the other room. My other children are at school." *Why am I telling him the truth? Why didn't I tell him someone else was here, or that I'm expecting company very soon? Anything to make him believe I'm not alone and vulnerable.*

"Anyone else here?" he sneers, stretching to look into the living room.

"Uh . . . well, no, but my husband will be back any minute," I lie. *Nice girls don't lie. Is it wrong to lie at a time like this? Why am I so accommodating? I should have made up some story to distract him. There must be something I can do, but I don't know what it is. Please, Lord, help me. Don't let him hurt Amy or me.*

Grasping at minute particles of hope, I pray the telephone will ring so I can grab it and cry for help, just like they do in the movies. But it never rings. I will a neighbor to drop by for coffee, but no one comes.

"Where's the bedroom?" he snickers with piercing eyes.

"That way." I point toward the den area that leads to the master bedroom. *Why me?* I agonize.

With the blade of the knife nudged menacingly on my shoulder, he tightens his grip on my arm and pushes me toward the bedroom. *Is this it? Have I signed my own death certificate? Will I die at the hands of a rapist?*

I silently quote the twenty-third psalm. Over and over I repeat, "Yea, though I walk through the valley of the shadow of death, I will fear no evil, for Thou art with me." I *am* in the valley of the shadow of death. And my child, who is sleeping in the next room is as helpless as I.

Still grasping my arm, he shoves me into the bedroom, then reaches back and closes the door. He steers me over to the bed. *Lord, please make him put that knife away. It is scaring me to death. Will he rape me first and then stab me, or will he scratch me up, maybe dismember me, and stuff me into the closet? Does he see me shaking? Is he even capable of a simple human emotion?*

"Take off your clothes," he storms.

I decide to appeal to his sense of decency. "Please don't do this," I beg. "I'm a Christian, a child of God."

He doesn't respond. I wonder if he even heard me. "Do it now!" he bellows.

I do as he says. I don't want Amy to hear him and wake up. In that moment of truth, when it comes to losing my dignity or losing my life, my one goal is survival.

Releasing my arm so I can undress, he steps back and scans the setting. The door to Amy's bedroom that links to ours is slightly ajar. He moves toward it. *Oh, no! Don't go in there. My baby is there. Please God, don't let him go into Amy's room. Amy, darling, be asleep. Don't make a sound, my sweet. Everything is just fine.*

He shuts her door. I start undressing, slowly and precisely, hoping he will have second thoughts or find me unappealing. Maybe the scar from the abdominal surgery I had last year will repulse him. It doesn't. There is no escaping the humiliation and degradation I feel at being forced to stand completely naked before this vile, amoral stranger, but submissively I obey. The clothes I had so carefully picked out to wear today lie at my feet, crumpled in a heap.

Desperate, I try to bargain. I tell him I have a kidney and liver disease. No response. I talk about my husband again, confirming my lie that he will be returning any moment. I tell him my other two children will be coming home from school. He continues to stare and registers no emotion. Holding the knife on me, he reaches behind him and takes a T-shirt out of the bureau drawer. I am indignant. *My God, what does he think he's doing? He can't do that. That's my husband's T-shirt. How dare he take something that isn't his!* That was just the beginning.

"Climb on the bed," he commands ruthlessly.

Acquiescing, I ease onto the edge of the bed. My heart is pounding so hard I fear it might explode in my chest cavity. He twists the T-shirt around my head and ties it into a knot, blindfolding me. The room is pitch black. Now I am defenseless as well as powerless. I can't see the knife. I can't see where he is. I can't see what he's doing. But I can still feel his cold, glazed eyes watching me. Silent hysteria rages throughout the core of my being.

My hopes of a miracle dissipate in the reality of the moment. I have screamed, but no one has come. The phone hasn't rung. Nick hasn't come back. No one has stopped by for coffee. There is no way of escape. Suddenly, I realize I have one last defense. This merciless intruder may have choreographed everything else in this afternoon nightmare, but there is one part of me he cannot touch. He cannot dominate my soul. He may brutalize my body but he cannot tell me what to think or feel or believe. There is a part of me he can never victimize unless I choose to let him.

Lord, if You have ever heard my prayers, please hear me now! I don't know what else to do. This man may try to kill me and harm Amy. I am not ready to die and she is an innocent child. I want to watch my children grow up. There are so many things I want to do. Nick and I have plans. Please help me. I am putting myself in Your hands and I am going to trust You to save me from this wicked man.

Miraculously, in the midst of trembling and fear, I am flooded with peace. At that moment, I accept that I am going to be raped, but know that I am not going to die. I will live.

The bed moves. He crawls toward me. I feel his heavy breaths on my neck. Cringing with disgust I close my eyes tightly, even though I can't see. I stiffen with repulsion. I think I am going to be sick and swallow hard to suppress the nausea. *Oh, God, I hate this.*

Minutes seem like hours. Finally, it is over.

That was in 1979. Since then, I have learned many things about myself, about being a victim, and about overcoming, facing reality and taking charge of my life. I have survived. I have grown. I have learned that nice girls *do* get raped, and by sharing the totality of my trauma, I want to offer encouragement and insight to my fellow victims, their families, friends, pastors, counselors and nurses. Most of all I want to give hope. I want to suggest, based on my experience, what you might do if it happens to you or someone you know and love.

2

Where Do I Go From Here?

The rustle of the bedcovers and shifting of the mattress indicated the rapist was ready to leave.

"Don't move for ten minutes," he sneered. "I'll be watching the house for several days. If I see police cars here, I'll be back to finish you off."

The chilling warning worked. Degraded and still blindfolded, I froze, stifling my breath out of fear. An eerie stillness filled the room. *Where is he? What is he doing? Is he going to stab me now?* I wondered.

I heard the click of the door and I knew he had turned the knob. Moments later I heard his footsteps outside the bedroom window. He seemed to be running between the houses toward the street. Just then I heard what sounded like a car or van tear down the street. *Has someone been waiting for him? Is he really gone? Is it over?*

Slowly I removed my husband's T-shirt from around my head. The trauma of the assault heightened, and I was beyond the capacity to endure any longer. Exhausted, but also relieved at being alive, I began sobbing uncontrollably. Tears of humiliation and shame cascaded down my cheeks, and I groped for the bedcovers to hide my disgrace. Collapsing back on the bed I felt emptied of all dignity and respect.

Suddenly I panicked. *Oh, no. It's nearly time for Nicole and Lisa to come home. I can't let them find me like this.* Frantic that they would see me in this disheveled and fragile condition, I forced myself to think about what to do next. There was no time to waste wishing it hadn't happened or sitting numbly submerged in self-pity. Within minutes I had to pull myself together and greet the girls like I always did.

Cautiously, I crept off the bed. As I hobbled in front of the dresser, I was horrified by what I saw in the mirror. Wild alarm flamed in my eyes. My face was ashen. It was obvious that something had shattered me. I left my clothes crumpled in a heap on the floor as I reached for a robe and wondered how I could hide my trauma. Nicole, eight years old, was particularly sensitive and would immediately realize something was terribly wrong.

Bewildered and in shock, I fumbled as I put on the robe, and then I hobbled to the kitchen table. In a blur of confusion, I flipped through the yellow pages in an attempt to call Nick at the golf course. Gasping through spills of tears on the phone book, I again panicked. I didn't know which course he was playing. I was like a helpless child, desperately needing someone to tell me what to do next. *How can this have happened to me? Nice girls don't get raped!*

What Next?

Never before had I experienced the sheer terror I felt that afternoon. I couldn't organize my thoughts. I couldn't focus on what to do. Sitting limp in the dining room, I felt deserted and alone, abandoned by God and mankind. Robbed of my dignity, I had been thrown to a salivating lion to be devoured. Something inside me died that day.

Pete. That's it — I'll call Nick's brother. Maybe he will know which course Nick is playing. They often played golf together, and by some miracle maybe Pete could tell me where Nick might be. I didn't want to bother Pete, but I was desperate. Through blurred eyes I picked up our address book and searched for the number. When I finally found it, I dialed.

"Good afternoon, Marshall Enterprise," a receptionist

answered.

"Uh . . . may I . . . could I please speak with Mr. Maher?" I asked in a voice I didn't recognize.

"Who's calling, please?" she said brightly. Click. I was on hold for what seemed hours.

"Hi, Jen, what's up?" Pete said cheerfully.

"Uh . . . Pete, uh . . . do you know. . ." My voice trailed. I couldn't get the words out.

"Jen, what's the matter?" Pete's tone abruptly changed from cheerful to concerned. "You sound different." He, like Nicole, had always been sensitive to my feelings. Today was no exception.

"Uh . . . Pete, do you know where Nick might be playing golf?" I somehow managed to utter.

I hated alarming Pete, but I couldn't explain. He didn't know where Nick might be. After saying good-bye, my heart was heavy. *Poor Pete. I do hope he will forgive me.*

I don't know what I would have done on that nightmarish afternoon if the girls hadn't been due home from school. Perhaps I would have wandered around the house in a daze for hours. As it was, I finally was able to call for help in spite of shock and fragmented rationale.

Four Simple Steps

The trauma of sexual assault often blocks the ability of a rape victim to think clearly. I needed someone to tell me what to do next. The Sexual Assault Prevention Training Guide states: "Many people have no idea what steps they should take or the activities to be avoided immediately following a sexual assault."[1]

Although the circumstances surrounding sexual assaults are different for each victim, four simplified steps remain the same:

1. Get safe.
2. Get help.
3. Get care.
4. Get support.

Severe psychological trauma combined with fear can be paralyzing to the rape victim. She most likely will be in crisis and struggling to function. Yet she must make some decisions. Concentrating on the above simplified steps will help give a central focus to a clouded mind.

Personal Needs Versus Evidence

After a sexual assault, a woman usually has a strong urge to shower, bathe, douche, wash her hands, brush her teeth, wash her hair and use the toilet. She will be anxious to rid herself of the unclean feelings that nearly always follow rape. Deviant acts may have been performed on her or she may have been forced to perform them, and that will compound her feelings of being tainted and dirty.

But, as hard as it may be, she *must* wait to cleanse herself until after the medical examination and police procedures are completed. To do otherwise can destroy evidence that will be vital if there are court proceedings later. If you are the victim, it may be helpful for you, while you are waiting to wash, to concentrate on your mental and physical health. You are the *survivor* of a sexual assault, and you have the right to whatever medical treatment is needed to aid in your recovery and to whatever police protection and follow-up is appropriate.

The only thing I knew for sure was not to take a shower. Nick and I had watched a TV movie about a rape victim a few months earlier and I remembered that part, but that was all. To convict a rapist, irrefutable evidence is needed to support the fact that the victim was indeed raped.

The victim must realize the full importance of this because, unfortunately, the wait to wash could result in even further humiliating ordeals. According to *Time* magazine, one victim, Linda, a Houston nurse, said, "I was on my period and had a tampon embedded deep inside. I had to sit and talk to a policeman with dried semen all over my face."[2]

We will discuss the gathering of evidence more fully in chapter 5 when we talk about reporting the rape to the authorities.

Results of Fear

The victim of sexual assault will have certain, normal functions taking place in her body as a result of fear. According to David Viscott, M.D., in *The Language of Feelings,* "Anxiety is the *fear* of being hurt or of losing something. Whether the fear is real or imagined, it *feels* the same. Anxiety varies from the mild apprehension of someone testing the temperature of the water before going swimming to the disorganized panic of a person unable to control his bodily functions. Between these two extremes are feelings of being fearful, scared, edgy, jittery, concerned, worried, helpless, insecure, uptight, nervous, having cold feet, getting the shakes — all degrees of a feeling of uncertainty over one's personal safety."[3]

Studies show that when we are faced with fear, whether it's a roaring lion or a squeaking mouse, physiological changes take place in our bodies. Viscott goes on to say, "When you're exposed to a threat, your body responds by releasing powerful stimulating hormones into the bloodstream. These hormones make the heart beat more strongly and more rapidly and also direct blood flow to where it's needed most. In a time of stress the blood supply is usually diminished to the abdomen and the skin, and is increased to the muscles. Most of the physical symptoms of anxiety — cold feet, butterflies in the stomach, sweating, dilation of the pupils of the eyes and skin pallor — are caused by these hormones."

Self-talk often can be beneficial in reducing anxiety. Repeating phrases like "Relax now; just breathe slowly; it's O.K. now" to herself will help the rape victim's breathing and blood flow to return to normal. Putting on a sweater or wrapping herself in a light blanket will help bring her chilled body back to its normal body heat.

The rape victim also can help stabilize her emotions by repeating stress-coping thoughts like "I'm going to be all right. I've survived. It's over now. He's gone. I'm safe." Repeating statements like these will center her thinking and help relieve the fragmentation. The energy she uses to gain a focus may reduce further hysteria.

The Next Steps

Besides taking care of her personal needs, a rape victim must think through the following questions:

1. Who can I call for emotional support?
2. Should I report the assault to the police?
3. Where can I go for medical help?
4. What about legal procedures?
5. What are my rights?

Often, making the initial decision will determine the next step. For instance, reporting the assault will lead to a police investigation, which may lead to a suspect, which may lead to legal proceedings, and so forth.

No one is ever prepared for the gripping horror of the reality of rape. But if the fears of the unknown are replaced with knowledge, the victim will have a better chance of proceeding in a beneficial way for herself.

3

Who Should She Call for Emotional Support?

Determining the right person to call for emotional support is an important decision. Although the rape victim may have many friends from whom she can pick, it is vital that she choose an empathetic person. Knowing she has someone dependable at her side will help ensure a sense of safety and sanity. It would be helpful for that person to stay with her during the after care, to be supportive and to listen as the necessary steps are taken.

According to *A Book About Sexual Assault,* the person she calls should be someone:

1. she finds easy to confide in;
2. she trusts to keep in confidence any details she does not wish to share with others;
3. who will be understanding and not judgmental;
4. who can respect her decisions and who will help her decide what is best for *her;*
5. who can be depended on to be called whenever needed;
6. she feels can deal with people like policemen, doctors, social workers, lawyers, etc., should she find it difficult.[1]

It isn't as important for the support person to be a long time friend as it is that she be a close, compassionate confidante. In this crisis, the victim will be sensitive to the actions and attitudes expressed by the support person as well as those expressed by others who come into her immediate contact, including her family. If these people are loving and responsive, she will be aware of their compassion. If they are condemning (for example, if they indicate they feel she is guilty of inviting the rape), she will detect their questioning of her character, and the experience will be even more traumatic for her. Since her value has been lessened already in her own mind, she desperately needs acceptance, assurance and affirmation from those around her.

If you should happen to be the support person called, remember that decisions must be made and the victim needs your help with those, but she should not be pressed for details of the rape or of her feelings. Your sensitive heart will allow her to describe her experience and express her feelings when she feels ready to speak. Allowing her to begin making her own decisions will encourage her and will be a stepping stone in the right direction. Proceed slowly, but consistently, taking one thing at a time. Always bear in mind her temporary fragility.

In my case, I had an interim support person who came to my rescue. Immobilized with fear, I was nearly non-functioning and knew I needed someone with me in my helplessness.

Somehow I gained courage to call my private physician. My doctor urged me to come to his office, but I knew I needed someone to drive me. Who could I ask? Who could I trust? Most of my friends worked. My mind went blank, yet I knew it was impossible for me to cope with the responsibility of driving a car.

Then the Lord brought Marilyn to my mind. Yes, maybe I would call Marilyn. She loved me and wouldn't ask questions. She worked part time, and I hoped this was her day off. She had been a faithful friend for many years, and I knew her number by heart. Her eldest daughter, Carol, babysat for us through the years and was presently staying at her parents' house while her husband was overseas.

"Carol, it's Jennifer," I managed to whisper. "Is your Mom home?"

"No, she's at work. I'm alone here with the baby," she replied.

"Is . . . is Sharon there?" I continued. Maybe her sister could come down.

"No, Sharon's not here either. What's the matter?" Carol inquired. "Are you sick? You sound like you don't feel well."

"Uh . . . no, uh . . . yes. Well, never mind. Thanks anyway. Good-bye," I said, dropping the receiver to my shoulder and wondering what to do next.

"Wait, Jennifer, do you want *me* to come down?" she blurted out, sensing my panic.

"No, that's O.K. You have your baby to care for," I answered as normally as I could.

"Jennifer, wait. Grandma Keller's at the front door. Wait. I'm coming over right now. She can stay here with the baby," she said, hanging up before I could protest.

Still in my robe, I went to open Amy's door to check on her. She was sound asleep. Shuffling over to her, I reached over and turned her angelic face to me, gently pushing the covers back. She fluttered her blue eyes sleepily and grinned. *Thank God she's been spared this afternoon nightmare.*

I sat Amy up and began putting her shoes on her. When I heard a knock at the back door, I pulled up the crib rail and made my way to the door, clinging to the furniture as I went.

Carol stood on the back step unsuspecting of the crisis on the other side of the door, or so I thought. I felt cruel, burdening her with my desperation.

Stunned at the sight of me in a bathrobe in the middle of the day, she hugged me and then waited for my next move. I told her we had to get out of the house quickly. Without questioning me, she took charge.

"Jennifer, you go get dressed and I'll finish with Amy," she said decisively.

Wandering into the den toward the master bedroom, I felt vacant.

I dreaded going back into the bedroom, and I stopped in front of the half-open door. *I can't do this,* I silently screamed. *I just can't!* Again, the nausea. My throat tightened. "I'll have to. The girls will be here any minute," I told myself.

Once in the bedroom, I walked straight to the closet without looking at the bed. I couldn't think what to wear, so I picked up the wrinkled clothes I had unwillingly dropped minutes ago and redressed.

"Carol, I have to get to Dr. Cantwell's office," I whispered as I returned to the living room. "We have to leave right now."

Thinking I was sick, Carol looked perplexed. I knew she was very concerned about what had happened, but she did not ask questions. She kindly expressed her love and willingness to do for me whatever I needed. We headed for the back door.

I glanced about the yard, up and down the sidewalk and down the street. Although Carol's car was parked by the side of the house, it seemed far away. *All that open space. I'll never make it. I can't.*

But I knew that, in order to get to the car, I would have to go that short distance. Taking a deep breath, I flew down the back steps, out the gate and jumped inside the car. I locked the door behind me as fast as my trembling fingers would work. Carol followed close behind with Amy.

After piling into the car, we picked up Nicole and Lisa at the nearby elementary school and rushed to the doctor's office ten minutes away. For some reason, during the harried ride, I mouthed to Carol, "I was raped." Aghast, she turned to me as if to say something, then suddenly realized Nicole and Lisa were peering over the back of the seat. She didn't say a word, but nodded that she understood. I was relieved she didn't visibly display her shock and disbelief.

Months later, Carol confided that by the time she got to my house that fateful day, she *knew* I had been raped. As she drove the short distance down the hill to my house, she heard the words, "Jennifer's been raped." Even as she heard them, she thought, *No, that can't be true.* Then, when I mouthed them, confirming her fear, she said it was as if the Lord had prepared her for the crisis situation ahead.

After she got me to the doctor's office, Carol's help continued. She took all three girls back to her house. Her sensitivity to my need was a great support.

At the doctor's office, after the police came, I was able to call Jody to be with me. She stayed for the remainder of the day and late into the night. Though there were others I could have called, my thoughts settled on her. In spite of the newness of our relationship, we had a bond. Jody was trustworthy and I had always felt comfortable in her presence. Her self-control and dignity reminded me of my beloved grandmother, and this day I felt especially loved as she demonstrated her compassion. I knew I had made the right choice.

Jody stayed at my side, giving me support during those first difficult days, through the following months and even years later. She has proven to be a faithful friend.

Once the rape victim decides who to call, and calls that person, she has taken the first step on the long journey to recovery, just as I was able to do. The loving assurance that she is no longer alone better equips the victim to face what lies ahead.

4

Where Should She Go for Medical Care?

Carol cautiously but swiftly drove the girls and me to Dr. Cantwell's office. We wound around the parking structure and finally found a space for the car. Carol carried Amy, and I took the hands of the older girls. Silently we walked through the hallway to the door of the office. With the girls hanging on to me for dear life, I felt more like I was going to the guillotine than for medical care. Fearful of seeing someone I knew, I tried to be as inconspicuous as possible by walking with my head down and arms turned inward.

Though still dazed, I somehow made it to the reception window where I was greeted with a cheery smile as I signed in. I attempted to return the welcome, hoping the receptionist would think this a routine visit. Even so, questions congested my mind. *Does she know the real reason I'm here? Did Dr. Cantwell tell her what happened?*

Glancing about the familiar room, I hesitated while deciding where to sit, but before I could slip into a chair, the tall, dark-haired secretary called my name and we started for Dr. Cantwell's office.

"Dr. Cantwell will be with you in a few moments," she offered.

"Uh . . . thank you," I shakily uttered.

Dr. Cantwell met us in the hall and we talked briefly. He suggested I try to call someone to come and be with me during the examination. I phoned home to see if Nick had returned. I knew it was unlikely since it was only 3:30 and he had said he wouldn't see me until dinnertime. *Only 3:30? How can this be? Was it only a little over an hour ago that I was standing in my back yard singing in the bright sun? Now my world looks so bleak.*

The examining room was not quite ready so I went back toward the reception area. When I opened the door, the girls all bounded over to me, happily hugging me and smothering my face with kisses. To my adoring daughters, I seemed the same. Carol followed and suggested she take them to her house where they would be more comfortable and could play. I hugged them each good-bye, telling them I would be fine and would see them in a little while.

Once they were all out the door I collapsed into a chair around the corner next to the wall.

Oh, that lady over there. Does she see me? She mustn't see me. I won't make a sound. I know if she looks at me, she'll know. I felt like a sign was taped across my chest with big, bold letters on it: RAPED.

After what seemed hours but was only about fifteen minutes, a professional-looking woman in a crisp white uniform stepped into the waiting room with a chart in her hand.

"Jennifer Maher?" she called. "Would you please come with me?"

I froze, wishing this wasn't really happening. Again she called, this time a little louder, "Jennifer Maher, are you here?"

Oh, dear, she's waiting for me to respond. I don't want to be here. But I can't go home. What will they do to me? I don't think I can handle this confusion alone. Oh, Nick, why aren't you here holding me in your strong arms telling me everything will be all right?

Submissively, I trailed after the briskly moving figure in white. She introduced herself as Barbara, the nurse, and took me back to the check-in station.

"Mrs. Maher, is this a routine visit?" Barbara kindly asked.

Well . . . uh . . . no, well, sort of," I mumbled.

She must be puzzled. Here I am, a grown woman, and I can't even give her a straight answer as to why I'm here today.

Sensing my uneasiness, Barbara responded, "Well, that's O.K., dear. I'll just go ahead and check your blood pressure."

As she tightened the cuff around my arm, I wondered how high my blood pressure would register. *Does she notice I'm trembling uncontrollably? Can she tell by my faint voice I've just been through a terrible experience?*

"Now, that's good," she replied professionally, folding up the cuff. "Let's hop on the scale and check your weight."

Usually I dreaded weighing, but today the size of my battered and bruised body was not a priority.

Through cracking voice, I managed to tell her I had talked with Dr. Cantwell earlier and he said to come immediately to the office. I had not intended to confide in Barbara, but because of her warmth, I found myself blurting out my ordeal. After listening intently, she revealed to me that she had been raped a number of years ago when at the beach. I was surprised to discover she, too, was a rape victim. Once again, but oh so briefly, the clouds parted and the Son shed a ray of His light on me. God placed that nurse there that day just for me.

Barbara must have recovered enough to go on with her life because she had laughed and joked when I had been in over the past months. She actually seemed happy, not at all like I would expect a rape victim to be. It didn't seem possible that I, too, could recover from my crisis or ever celebrate life again.

Once in the examination room, Barbara instructed me to undress and put on the white paper gown, then told me Dr. Cantwell would be in soon. Alone again, I wondered what would happen next.

Laying my clothes on the dressing room chair, I looked long at what had been a perfectly coordinated outfit. Then suddenly I never wanted to see them again. All I wanted to do was take a shower and wash away this dirtiness and stench. *Did Barbara smell the odor? Why does the doctor have to examine me to verify I was raped? I wouldn't say I was raped*

*if I wasn't. Can't they just take my word for it? Oh, God, I
hope this is over soon.*

Sitting on the cold, hard, examination table, I glanced
about at the sterility of the room. I couldn't believe I'd have
to endure further degradation. *They at least could add some
warmth to these rooms. And they leave you in this little
cubicle all alone for so long.* I remembered when I was the
nurse in this office several years earlier, how many countless
times I had put patients into this room, and I shuddered. *Did
I ever check in a rape victim? Did I help, or did I hinder?*

Suddenly, the door opened wide and Dr. Cantwell stood
near.

. "Hello, Jenny," he said matter-of-factly, but compassionately. "Are you all right?"

An icy chill swept through my body. I could hardly
swallow. *No,* I wanted to scream, *I'm not all right! I'm scared
and ashamed and I don't understand why this has happened.
I've never done anything to hurt anyone.* Or had I? Was I
being punished?   In spite of tension, I managed to answer
with deceptive calmness, "Hi, Dr. Cantwell."

"Jenny, I'm going to examine you for any injuries sustained
during the assault. This will take just a few minutes," he
gently assured me.

The only visible mark I had was a large bruise on my
left upper arm where the rapist had gripped me. Each time
I looked, the purple discoloration had grown uglier. I found
myself shivering with disgust.

Dr. Cantwell then explained he had to do a pelvic examination and obtain a specimen for the slide to prove I had
been raped. *What? Proof? Good Lord, can't they see what a
mess I am? Yes, I was raped. What more do they need? How
much more humiliation do I have to go through?*

After the exam, Dr. Cantwell went out of the room to
examine the slide under a microscope. Again I was left alone
with the stark reality of my nightmare. Staring blankly at the
four white walls, I wondered what had happened to my
picture-postcard-perfect day. The doctor returned a few minutes
later and confirmed my account. "Well, thank God," I muttered
under my breath with an edge of sarcasm.

Where Should a Victim Go for Medical Care?

If you have experienced this depth of degradation, then you know more than you care to about human suffering. If you haven't, you know you never want to. Yet, you need to realize that proper medical care by trained staff will help decrease further emotional or physical trauma.

Immediately after a rape, the victim is usually in shock, and probably will be unaware of injuries sustained during the assault. However, even if there are no obvious cuts, lacerations, bruises or other wounds, it is imperative for her to be treated medically. Tests for pregnancy and sexually transmitted diseases are necessary to insure her personal health and well being. Photographs of injuries and appropriate collection and preservation of medical evidence are required for possible later prosecution of the rapist.

Points to Consider

When making the decision to seek medical care, there are a number of questions that need to be considered:

1. What community services are available?
2. What is the fee? Is this service taken care of by victim's compensation or health insurance, or is there state reimbursement?
3. What are the hours of the facility? Is it 24-hour service or by appointment only?
4. Will the rape victim feel comfortable in the environment?[1]

Emergency room personnel, the police or the victim's private physician can provide guidance in obtaining the medical care she needs. One thing she should do is take extra clothing in the event that what she is wearing will need to be kept as evidence.

A Private Physician

Going to the victim's own private physician has advantages and disadvantages for her.

Advantages: She will be surrounded by familiar faces. Also, the office personnel may show her more dignity and provide more privacy than she would receive in a hospital emergency room.

Disadvantages: Private doctors' offices do not often have rape victims come in for treatment. They may not have the necessary facilities to collect medical evidence. The doctor may not be aware of the specialized understanding a victim needs in order to make the medical examination easier to endure. The staff may not be aware of the importance of appropriate support responses. And finally, depending on when the rape occurs, finding an office open at the time the victim needs care may be difficult.

Another disadvantage is that the private physician may be unwilling to testify should the case go to court. He may not want to take time away from his practice to appear at the trial, since giving medical testimony may take several days. The victim may want to question the doctor before receiving treatment so she will have full knowledge of his position. If she is unable to make these inquiries, her support person should do it for her. Questions also should be asked regarding financial arrangements, since private care can be quite expensive.

Community Clinic

The rape victim may prefer a community clinic that offers 24-hour service. In this environment the atmosphere is likely to be relaxed and usually there are less accusatory attitudes toward a victim of sexual assault. Also, in the clinic setting, doctors, nurses, and social workers may use more of a collaborative team approach, respecting each others' contributions. This rapport enhances the care of the patient.

Emergency Room

In recent years care in hospital emergency rooms has become specialized for sexual assault cases. Often, the staff has been specifically trained to care for the sensitive needs of rape victims due to their severe shock and trauma. This reduces further humiliation as much as possible during the remaining medical procedures.

If a rape victim chooses to be treated in an emergency room, her first contact will be the supervising nurse or admitting clerk in the waiting room area. The victim will be asked some simple questions such as: Why are you here? What is your name? Address? Age and occupation? In light of the terrifying shock she has just survived, these questions may seem completely irrelevant, but they provide necessary information for her medical chart.

She will be handed consent forms which will allow the hospital staff to acquire medical evidence, and she may request help in completing these forms. Although she does not have to give all of the details to the nurse, it is absolutely imperative that the nurse be told about the rape so the victim will receive the proper medical treatment. A social worker or medical advocate may be enlisted to assuage the victim's fears as well as to help in other ways. A rape victim has the right to be accompanied through each medical procedure by the support person of her choice. She also has the right to total privacy during the examination, and may request that everyone leave the room other than the needed hospital personnel.

Prior to the examination, questions will be asked about the assault. It is essential the victim's violations be described in detail, such as vaginal intercourse, oral copulation, anal intercourse or any other acts, however deviant. This probably will be unpleasant, but it isn't necessary to hide her inner turmoil by holding back tears or by suppressing emotions.

The victim also will be asked to sign another consent form stating her agreement to release records of the medical examination to the police and to her attorney's office. These records will become part of her case file and will be used during prosecution of the rapist. The signing of this form does not mean she is required to prosecute, but it is necessary for records.

The victim's blood pressure, temperature, pulse and medical history will be taken. After the paperwork is completed, she will be instructed to undress. It is at this point her clothing may be taken and may not be returned until after the trial. She will be asked to comb pubic hair onto a small piece of paper. The loose hairs will be put into an envelope and kept as evidence. She may be asked to pull hairs from her head; these will be put into a separate envelope.

Next, she will be given a general examination. The doctor will listen to her heart and lungs, press on her back and abdomen, examine her breasts and check for general signs of injury. Any marks, scratches, bruises, lumps or bumps will be noted on her chart. If she has any specific pains or soreness, these should be mentioned. What may seem insignificant to the patient can be very important from a medical standpoint.[2]

Another part of the exam, which may be particularly humiliating at this time, is the pelvic exam, also referred to as an internal exam. Lying on the examining table with feet high up in stirrups and a small drape covering the lower torso can be distressing to any woman. But after a sexual assault, this position can be extremely upsetting to the victim, causing her to lose control of her emotions. Or she may fight back her tears while reliving the violation she experienced during the rape. These feelings are normal. It may be of comfort to the victim to have her support person with her during this delicate time. If she is unable to ask the doctor to give her a few moments to collect herself, her support person may intervene on her behalf.

The victim may find it helpful to count to five slowly as a relaxing technique. Concentrating on a particularly happy time, asking questions, or squeezing the hand of her support person also may help her relax during the exam. She can ask for whatever kind of support she needs, though some victims find this impossible due to their traumatized emotions.

During the pelvic exam the doctor will check the genital area for tears, cuts, bruises or other signs that indicate force. Samples will be taken from the vagina to check for sperm cells. If sperm cells are present, it is recorded whether they are alive and moving. The degree of movement indicates how recently the rape occurred.

At this time the doctor may request fingernail scrapings and a Wood's lamp exam. Fingernail scrapings can help identify the rapist or locate the exact place of the crime. If the victim scratched or touched her attacker, any material found underneath her fingernails can be matched to the rapist, his clothing or objects found at the crime scene.

The Wood's lamp exam is done in a darkened room. Any semen left on clothing or on the body will glow. This test only suggests that the clothing be examined more carefully; the fluorescence itself is not evidence.[3]

The pubic hair exam mentioned earlier also may be done at this time.

Tests for Venereal Disease

Although venereal diseases are spread through different forms of sexual contact, it is reported that less than 10 percent of rape victims acquire these diseases. The two that are most commonly transmitted through sexual assault are *gonorrhea* and *syphilis*. Either can result in serious consequences.

Testing for gonorrhea should be done ten days to two weeks after the rape has occurred. If the test is positive, the victim will be treated with high doses of penicillin for fourteen days. She needs to be certain testing is done in all areas of sexual contact with the assailant — vagina, anus, mouth, throat, etc. Symptoms are practically unnoticeable in women — 80 percent are asymptomatic — but these tests should *never* be overlooked.

The symptoms for syphilis are also difficult to detect in women. A rape victim must be tested approximately six weeks after the rape and then again two weeks later with a VDRL blood test. If the test results are positive, the treatment is antibiotics.

Other Possible Problems

Trichomona: A vaginal infection with symptoms of discharge, itching, irritation and a foul odor. The medical treatment for this is a prescription for Flagyl tablets.

Genital herpes: This viral disease, a close relative of the cold sore, occurs in the genital area and is often very painful.

Although no cure has been discovered yet for this sometimes chronic condition, medical treatment can alleviate the tenderness. Herpes frequently recurs.

Vaginal infection: If symptoms of irritation or soreness remain after the first 24 hours, the victim may have a vaginal infection. She needs a follow-up examination one week after the rape to be checked for this problem. Treatment usually consists of vaginal suppositories and/or antibiotics.

Lacerations: When the victim sustains lacerations, a tetanus shot is generally recommended if she has not had one in the last five years.

Body lice (crabs): Itching around the pubic area may indicate body lice which attach to the hair shaft. Treatment involves bathing with a special solution, which can be bought over the counter (such as A2100, RID, or R & C shampoo), and washing of bed linens.

Scabies: Scabies are mites which burrow into the skin. Treatment consists of specialized washing of linens and bathing with Kwell which is a prescription medication.

Genital warts: Sometimes called condyloma, these viral warts can surround the genital area and, without proper treatment, can spread internally and cause serious complications. Medical care is necessary and usually consists of a series of podophyllin applications to the warts. If there is a pregnancy, a Caesarean section is frequently recommended to protect the baby.

AIDS: Although it is rare for a rape victim to test positive for Human Immuno Deficiency virus (more commonly recognized as acquired immune deficiency syndrome or AIDS), that virus can be passed to the victim who *may* become a carrier. She *could* pass it to her husband who *could* test positive. For testing, some states have alternative antibody testing sites, or you can call a local health organization or AIDS organization. For more information, write:

APLA (AIDS Project of Los Angeles)
7362 Santa Monica Blvd.
West Hollywood, CA 90046

Pregnancy Testing

Although studies report pregnancy rarely results from rape, this issue needs to be addressed. There is a 4 percent risk of pregnancy if the rape victim is menstruating or pre-menstrual and a 10 percent risk if she is mid-cycle. She will be asked to provide a urine sample for a pregnancy test usually two weeks after the rape. New pregnancy tests are now on the market which are much more sensitive and show results seven to ten days past a possible conception. Doctors' offices, clinics and the hospital emergency room will offer the victim three options: the "morning-after pill," menstrual extraction, or postponement of pregnancy testing.

The morning-after pill: All aspects of taking this drug should be considered due to possible serious complications. This pill has a high hormone level similar to the birth control pill. Two pills must be taken within 72 hours of possible conception. In 12 hours, two more pills are taken. Since this method is not 100 percent effective in causing the expulsion of the product of conception and can cause birth defects, a consent form is frequently required stating the patient will have a follow-up abortion.[4] For further information on the danger of taking this pill, refer to *What the Rape Victim* [or anyone] *Should Know About the "Morning-After Pill,"* a booklet from Advocates for Medical Information, 2120 Bissonet, Houston, TX 77005.

Menstrual extraction: This is done *after* a positive pregnancy test. In this procedure the endometrium, the lining of the uterus, is suctioned out and checked for verification of conception.

Postponement of testing: This is the option of waiting to see if a period is missed. If so, the victim can then request a pregnancy test by her own doctor, a hospital emergency room, or a free clinic. She can make further decisions based on the results of that test.[5]

If you are the victim, you need to know that, due to the legal, moral and spiritual ramifications of these procedures, it is important for you to discuss these options at length with your family, a close friend and your minister. Finally, seek God's wisdom and counsel before taking any of these actions.

Regardless of the circumstances of conception, what man meant for evil, God can work for good. His ways are not our ways. The following true story reveals the impact of these crucial decisions:

In the middle 1890s, Louise, a black girl of twelve, was raped by John, a white boy. A baby was conceived through this violent act. Louise's mother, who had a heart for God, refused to take matters in her own hands. Instead, she committed her daughter's pregnancy and unborn child unto the Lord's care. Nine months later, Ethel Waters was born, the famous gospel singer known especially for [her rendition of] "His Eye Is on the Sparrow."[6]

Follow-Up Visits

When the exam is complete, the victim will be instructed to return for the follow-up visits necessary to complete her treatment. During these visits further tests for venereal diseases and pregnancy will be administered. These visits can be made to the emergency room, to the victim's private physician, or to a free clinic. However, it is extremely important for the victim to make all the follow-up visits exactly as the doctor instructs her. They *must be made*.

The rape victim has just been through a nightmare. Besides the love and acceptance she needs from others, she will need to give herself permission to care for herself enough to see that she gets the physical care necessary. She needs to know that she can call the medical personnel, a rape hot line or a social worker for emotional support at any time while she is waiting for test results — or whenever she just needs a friend.

The Greatest Comfort

There will be times when even the victim's closest friends or the most capable people in the medical profession will not be able to minister to her deepest needs. At these times a gentle reminder of the friend we have in Jesus can bring a healing balm to her. Maybe you are just the right person to bring her to the greatest source of comfort there is. If so, take that step now. Point her to the God of all comfort and encourage her to rest in His healing arms for He is intimately familiar with all she's experiencing.

If you are the victim, and you have accepted Jesus Christ sometime during your life, then He is with you now. His constant presence and sustaining power in the midst of pain transcends all crises. By claiming His provision while facing further degradation through medical examinations, tests, poking and probing, you can count on the peace that passes all understanding to be your stronghold.

Psalm 31:2 reads:

> Incline Thine ear to me, rescue me quickly;
> Be Thou to me a rock of strength,
> A stronghold to save me.

5

Should She Report
the Incident to the Police?

Jennifer, do you want to report the rape to the police?" Dr. Cantwell asked matter-of-factly after meeting me in his office following the exam. I panicked at the thought of the rapist's threat to return if he saw any patrol cars around our house. Yet even in my confusion I experienced a sense of loyalty to other women. Would the rapist strike another unsuspecting woman, teen or child? I saw that my only hope to prevent that and see justice done was to report the crime and pray for his arrest. Yes, if that would keep him from assaulting other women, I definitely wanted to notify the police.

Astonished at my own decisiveness, I answered, "Yes, Dr. Cantwell, I want to report this."

Dr. Cantwell ushered me to the door and the receptionist guided me to a phone where I would have privacy and quiet.

My eyes were red and puffy from crying, so I had a hard time locating the number for the police division in the west Los Angeles area. I finally dialed, but reached the wrong precinct and had to start all over. My hands trembled as I dialed again.

"Seventeenth precinct, Sergeant Harris, can I help you?" the man asked gruffly.

"Uh . . . yes," I timidly said.

"Speak up, ma'am. I can't hear you," he barked.

"Yes, I want to report a rape," I said quietly, not wanting anyone to overhear.

"Ma'am, I can't hear ya. You'll have to speak louder," his voice boomed.

I can't talk louder. Everyone will hear me. Oh, Lord, help him hear.

"I want . . . I want to report a rape," I struggled to repeat with waning voice.

"What? Who was raped?" the officer shouted.

Frustration grew within as I tried to make myself understood without announcing my plight to the whole office.

My manner was subdued, but I spoke as clearly as I could manage and finally clarified to him why I was calling.

The officer told me I could choose to come to the police station, or they would send out an officer to my location to conduct the questioning. The movie I'd seen on TV about rape flashed vividly into my mind. I remembered that the victim had experienced endless harassment and humiliation in the impersonal setting of the police station. I didn't think I could bear sitting in a cold, unfeeling environment, being stared at by gawking strangers like a freak in a circus show. So I said, "Please send the detective to Dr. Cantwell's office."

I hung up the receiver and shuffled back to my hideaway seat in the corner of the reception area to wait for the officer to arrive. Alone and tormented both emotionally and spiritually, I felt separated from my surroundings, from mankind and from God. For the first time in my life I caught a minute glimpse of Christ's suffering for the world. Though I could hardly bear this blow life had dealt me, I knew He bore it all on Calvary's tree for me. What right did I have to sit crying in my sorrow and grief? My bruised and swollen arm couldn't begin to match his scourged and pierced body. There was no feeling or emotion in my agony that the King of Kings and Lord of Lords had not already suffered when He became sin for us.

As a child of God with His Word hid in my heart, I knew I wasn't forsaken. But I was emptied. My trauma had drained any reserve stamina. God would have to be my strength for what lay ahead.

Suddenly the office door flew open and two police officers boldly entered. One was young looking, with dark hair and a smooth face. The other one was older and taller, and appeared to be more experienced. Their guns and night sticks scraped black leather belts, causing the official odor of authority to permeate the room. *Do they see me hiding here, cringing in the corner? Can they tell I'm the rape victim?* Immediately they were ushered beyond the door into the back part of the office.

Holding my abdomen, I exhaled relief. *Oh, good. They're gone.* Like a fearful child, I wished for the questioning to be over even before it began.

A few moments later, Barbara once again called my name. This time, she directed me to Dr. Cantwell's office.

"Jenny," Dr. Cantwell began gently, "this is Officer Tenderella and Officer Blackwell. They want to talk with you. You can use my office while I see the rest of my patients."

Forcing myself to look at them, I noticed that the younger officer looked gentle and kind, like a sensitive big brother. The older man looked official and strong. They didn't look mean and condemning as I had feared they would be.

"Mrs. Maher, I'm Officer Tenderella," the older one said. "Would you like to have someone with you during this time of questioning?"

"Um . . . yes, I would like my husband to be here, but I haven't been able to reach him yet," I replied with deceptive calm.

"Is there someone else you would like to call in the meantime?" he continued.

These fellows are much different from what I expected. They seem sensitive and caring. Thank You, God. I don't think I could stand it if they were rude and demeaning.

At first my numb mind couldn't think of anyone, but then Jody's face appeared before me. Jody had become my friend the previous year when I was recovering from major surgery. I prayed she would be home when I called. I knew I desperately needed her, yet I had no idea what I would say when she answered the phone. After only two rings, I heard her familiar voice on the line. As calmly as possible, I asked if she could come to Dr. Cantwell's office. Thankfully, she asked no questions and arrived within fifteen minutes.

The receptionist brought Jody into the office, and like Carol, she didn't ask any questions. She simply came over immediately and took me in her arms. Sobbing like a baby, I buried my head on her shoulder to hide my shame. I didn't want to let go — it was such a relief to release some of my shame and confusion. She held and comforted me until I regained my composure.

I finally managed to tell Jody in a whisper that I had been raped. Momentarily she was stunned, and shook her head in horror. But Jody had stoical strength. She quickly recovered herself and then stood next to me with her arm about my shoulder throughout the questioning, comforting me in the especially hard places. I'll be eternally grateful for the acceptance and compassion she freely demonstrated to me on that dark day.

During the interrogation, Officer Tenderella kept assuring me I would be just fine. *How can he say that? How does he know I'm going to be fine when I don't even know that?* After an hour or so, the officers said they would have to finish the questioning at my house because they needed to search for evidence.

Dear God, I can't go back there. I can't. The rapist will see the police car and come back and kill me after they've gone. No, I won't go back.

In spite of my fears and my silent declaration, arrangements were made for the police to escort Jody and me to my house.

The Most Under-Reported Violent Crime

In 1982 there were over 77,000 reported rapes in the United States. This is a rate of approximately one reported rape every seven minutes, or 65 reported rapes for every 100,000 females. According to the U.S. Census Bureau, the National Opinion Research Center, and the FBI Uniform Crime Reports, the number of rapes actually committed is 3.5 to 10 times the number reported. In other words, authorities are notified of only one out of every ten rapes. However, the number of reported rapes has more than doubled over the past ten years. This increase may be attributed to a rise in the actual incidence of the crime, or to a change in victim willingness to report the violations, or to a combination of both factors.

The FBI Uniform Crime Reports also predict, "If there is no further increase in the rate at which rapes are committed, and if a woman is at risk for a minimum of 35 years of her life, and if the conservative 4 to 1 estimate of the number of actual rapes to the number of reported rapes is used, then the chances of a woman being raped sometime during her lifetime are about 1 in 11."

Reporting a rape is important for two reasons. First, only if it is reported to the authorities can it be investigated and the offender prosecuted. Second, the probability of the rape victim receiving therapy increases when the rape is reported. Gail Abarbanel, director of a nationally known Rape Treatment Center in Southern California, says, "To discourage women from reporting [these crimes to the authorities] is a bad message that implies the victim had a role in the rape."[1]

A variety of conditions can prevent or delay the victim's making a report. Many times a rapist's threats loom in the mind of his fragmented victim. Or the reactions of family and friends or the possibility of a humiliating trial can deter the report of a rape. But failure to report it indirectly grants the rapist license to commit the crime again.

Detective Steve Laird of the Los Angeles Police Department said during a phone interview, "We're seeing more willingness of the rape victim to report, particularly when interrogating officers explain how her reporting changes rape statistics. When that happens, communities and cities cannot ignore the urgent need for rape awareness and prevention programs and improved legislation."

Aspects of Reporting

If you are the victim, you are the only one who can decide whether to make an initial crime report and who will make it — yourself, your family, or a third party who reports anonymously. Here are some important facts to consider when making this decision.

Advantages

1. If you report the crime and the suspected rapist is caught and convicted, you have protected others from falling victim. Also, your reporting may help substantiate another survivor's report.
2. You will be eligible for Victims of Violent Crimes Compensation available in California. [Many other states also have victim assistance programs for obtaining financial reimbursement for medical services and professional counseling.]
3. You can request assistance throughout the trial process from victim advocates and/or crisis counselors.
4. [By reporting the crime,] you are exercising your rights.[2]

Disadvantages

1. It may be difficult for you to repeat your story continually to law enforcement officers and in court.
2. It may be emotionally difficult for you to relive the assault.
3. The district attorney has the right to decide whether to proceed with the case; although if he decides not to file, you are entitled to know why.
4. Fewer than one out of five cases goes to trial, and fewer result in conviction. Statistics can be discouraging, but remember — *no unreported* cases go to trial.

Preserving Evidence

Once the assault ends and you are safe, as mentioned in chapter 2 you will strongly desire to bathe, wanting to wash thoroughly all parts of your body that were abused. However, bathing must wait until after you are examined. This is necessary for the preservation of evidence and verification of the violation.

The Houston nurse we mentioned before had, in addition to the other things, a broken jaw, and the rapist had stuffed snowflake-shaped earrings into her vagina. The authorities had to know the truth about these.[3]

It is absolutely necessary also that evidence be collected as soon as possible after the rape. Otherwise, everyday activities, such as eating, drinking and elimination, can cause valuable evidence to be lost or destroyed. This is particularly significant if the victim was forced to perform oral sex. She must avoid taking any medication. She also must refrain from douching or even wiping the vaginal area until the verbal and physical examinations are completed. If seminal fluid is destroyed by douching, legal action may not be possible because of insufficient evidence.

Many victims are unaware of the value of saliva or even a shaft of hair. Scrapings from under the fingernails and toenails can be incriminating for the assailant. Moist or dried stains, or other lingering evidence on a victim's clothes, undergarments or skin may help lead to the rapist's arrest and conviction. In the case of mass murderer, Ted Bundy, who not only raped but maimed and murdered many of his victims, a pubic hair was discovered on an article of clothing worn by one victim. This tiny clue led to his arrest, and he was tried, convicted, and sentenced to execution.

Some rapists will go to great lengths to disguise themselves. In Northern California in the late 60s, one rapist poured a nauseous, foul-smelling mixture over himself before he assaulted his victims. Consequently, he acquired the nickname "Stinky." Carol Cravens, one of the estimated thirty women he has raped, reported during a TV interview by Tom Brokaw that her assailant had a terrible, vile odor. Because the offensive smell lingered on her, the police were able to identify the man immediately as the rapist called "Stinky." Unfortunately, to this day, he has not been caught.

Talking With the Police

When talking with the police, you have a right to understand what they are asking, why they are asking it and what it means. You also have the right to be aware of and understand what are appropriate and inappropriate questions. Keep in mind that the purpose of the police interrogation is to gather information.

Appropriate questions: The investigating officers will ask a number of questions that seem to have little to do with the rape. You should answer these to the best of your ability. Routine questions may include your age, address, phone number, place of employment, and other basic information. The officers will ask for the date, time and place of the rape and will also want a detailed description of the attack.

Inappropriate questions: Although you will be asked about your activities prior to the assault, you should not answer questions about your emotional or physical reactions at the time of the attack. Questions such as, Did you enjoy it? Did you climax? What were you wearing? etc., are all inappropriate and you are not required to answer them. Minnesota and other states have enacted "rape shield" statutes which prevent defense attorneys from probing a victim's past sexual experiences unless they can prove it is relevant. However, questions about your mental state may be asked in order to determine if a counseling referral is necessary. The officers' job is to help, not harass.

Still, some embarrassing and humiliating questions will have to be answered. Specifically, Did penetration occur? or, What sexual acts were forced upon you? These questions will determine which charges can be pressed, such as rape, rape with a foreign object, statutory rape, gang rape, etc. If only slight penetration occurred, an attempted assault charge will be pressed rather than a charge of assault. When giving this information, which may become the beginning of the basis for legal proceedings, the importance of accuracy cannot be overstated.

Victim Resistance Standard

The original law declaring rape a crime was enacted in 1872. It included a "victim resistance standard" which caused barriers to prevention and to effective treatment for the victim by the discriminatory attitudes it imposed. The origin of our rape laws corresponded to a time when women were considered property of men, or chattel, and rape was an extremely serious offense, punishable by long imprisonment or death. At that time women who reported rape were generally distrusted and the legal establishment sought protection against false charges and the conviction of innocent men. The law — and public attitudes — presumed that a virtuous woman would "by nature" resist to the point of death rather than allow the dishonor and the grave consequences her defilement would bring to herself and her family.

The Rape Treatment Center at Santa Monica Hospital Medical Center has treated more than two thousand victims. In the past, their findings showed the issue was not defense of honor. The issue was survival. Nonresistance to a rape does not a indicate a lack of virtue or character. Each person reacts differently when threatened with an attack. Some rape victims are unwilling to resist an assailant out of fear of death or serious injury to themselves or their loved ones. They assess the situation in the first seconds and decide that nonresistance is the safest strategy. Other victims are completely incapable of resisting because they are in a state of shock called "frozen fright." They literally are immobilized by fear and unable to resist.

No other violent crime requires any level of victim resistance for it to be a crime. Yet in rape, blame for the assault often was placed on the victim, particularly if she neglected to struggle for her life.

One victim's story illustrates the unfairness of the resistance standard. This woman was the last passenger on the bus and it was late at night. When the bus reached her stop, the driver locked the doors and she couldn't get off. She asked the driver to open the door, but instead of complying he said, "There is only one way you're getting off this bus."

The woman quickly looked outside hoping to summon help, but there was no one around. Again, she asked the driver to let her out of the bus. He refused. She pleaded, then attempted to open the door herself. He grabbed her, and she, immobilized by fear, was incapable of resisting the sexual assault. The assailant could not be prosecuted under California law because the state contained the victim resistance standard. Her psychological trauma was not enough — California women were expected to produce physical injuries proving resistance.

The Rape Treatment Center's founder and director, Gail Abarbanel, initiated an extension of the center's public education efforts, and they worked exhaustively for legislative reform. With the support of Assemblyman Mel Levine, Assembly Bill 2899 was drafted. Their combined work resulted in removal of the victim resistance standard, and a new definition of rape was adopted. January 1, 1981, marked the beginning of California rape victims being treated under the same standard as other victims of violent crime.[4] "A few states followed suit," said Mary Beth Roden, sexual assault specialist, Santa Monica Rape Treatment Center, in a phone interview, "but most don't have this standard."

After Making the Report

You may or may not be told that you have the right to read over the complete report and to request corrections of any misprints. In addition, you or your support person should obtain the names, badge numbers and telephone numbers of the investigating officers.

After you have reported your rape to the police, telling them everything you can, and the interrogation is completed, as soon as it becomes appropriate you should continue to pour out your thoughts and feelings by writing them in a journal. Writing in a free-flowing manner, with no thought or concern about punctuation or grammar, can provide much-needed release of haunting memories and troubling inner turmoil, and can be a stepping stone toward emotional as well as physical healing.

David writes in the psalms that when he kept silent about his sin, his body wasted away. Though rape is not your sin, or the result of your sin, still the temptation to harbor anger and hatred will be waiting at your heart's door. The releasing of feelings as honestly as possible on paper will help keep these sins from entering into your soul.

Further Investigation

A few days after you have made the initial police report, you will be contacted by the investigating detective for an interview. At this time you may request that a female investigator be present.

When I went through this part of my ordeal, I was not aware of victims' rights. I was frightened by the officers, not because they were frightening, but because of the grave psychological impact of the rape. Because of my fears, when Nick and I went to the police station a week after the rape, I feebly requested that a female officer do the questioning. A lady officer led me to a separate room for the interview, and that made it easier to answer her questions.

Sometimes after the initial interview, a rape victim will remember something more about either the assault or the assailant. If that happens with you, at that time, day or night, you should call and ask for the detective working on your case. If the investigator is unavailable, leave a message, requesting that your call be returned as soon as possible. Here again, the idea of keeping a journal may prove helpful. Not only is it therapeutic, but it also may jar your memory regarding an overlooked piece of information.

Another aspect of reporting the crime of rape is that you will be asked to cooperate with the police. They may ask you to come to the police station to view photographs (mug shots) of different men in an attempt to identify your assailant. This will be difficult and emotionally painful and may trigger a flood of memories.

You also may be asked to talk with a police artist so a composite drawing can be made. When a composite drawing of the "Night Stalker" killer was printed in the *Los Angeles Times,* he was identified by residents, leading to his arrest.[5]

Another facet of investigating the assault may include your being asked to return to the scene of the crime. You will be asked to point out any details that could prove to be evidence, no matter how remote that possibility may seem to you. Through the officers' specialized training they are able to detect even the slightest evidence.

Since my rapist was hooded, I was not asked to look at a line-up of men. An accurate identification would have been impossible. However, a rape victim who has seen the face of her assailant may be asked to carry out this difficult task. If you are asked to do this, I urge you to look to your close friends and family members and trust them to help you gain courage and strength. We need to convict rapists and get them into prison where they can receive treatment if we are going to reverse the rapid rise of this crime. But in order for this to happen, victims must cooperate with the authorities.

Line-ups are usually held in specially constructed rooms with reverse mirrors/windows. You will be able to see the suspect, but he won't see you. You are completely protected from his recognition and from any contact with him, other than viewing him through the glass.

California laws state that the suspect can be held for 72 hours. This may vary from state to state. If charges are not brought within three days, the authorities must release the suspect to avoid infringing on his rights. If charges are pressed, the judge posts bail, and in rare instances the suspect may be released on his own recognizance. If he's released, there is always the possibility of his raping again while awaiting trial. According to Mary Cecrle (CHE-cher-lee), Sexual Assault Victim Specialist with the Victim/Witness Assistance Program, Santa Ana, California, by the time a rapist is arrested, he has possibly committed the crime of rape thirteen times. Sometimes, when a rapist is out on bail, he rapes again, and he even maims or murders his victim.

If the suspect should be released, he will be instructed not to try to see or talk with you. Should he attempt any contact whatsoever, immediately call the detective. This type of contact can be used as the basis for placing the assailant back in custody.

Court Aspects

In the event a trial occurs, the case is usually decided by a jury based upon witnesses' testimonies and the physical evidence. In order for the suspect to be convicted, the jury must decide the suspect is guilty "beyond a reasonable doubt." In light of this, the defense attorney has the right to ask you questions. It may be suggested you are lying for some reason, and questions may be raised regarding your integrity. This is not an attempt to alter the truth, though it may prove difficult for you. Remember, you are the victim, and you are telling the truth. The defense attorney is merely doing his job in representing his client.

If the defendant is convicted, a sentence hearing may follow the trial. This is an open, public hearing which you may want to attend. If you do, you may want to contact the district attorney's office, your legal or medical advocate, your counselor, or the Victim-Witness Assistance Program in your area in order to feel more comfortable in the courtroom and have a better understanding of the criminal proceedings.

Legal Proceedings

Below is the usual order of events for legal proceedings. The list will vary from state to state depending on standard police procedure and from case to case depending on available evidence.

1. You file a crime report with law enforcement.
2. You may look at mug shots or assist in making a composite picture.
3. A suspect may be arrested.
4. You may be required to identify the suspect in a line-up.
5. Law enforcement presents the case to the district attorney.
6. You may be interviewed by the district attorney's office.
7. The district attorney decides whether there is enough admissible evidence to issue a formal complaint.
8. The suspect is arraigned in municipal court. (You may not be required to attend.)

9. If the suspect pleads not guilty, a preliminary hearing is set and you may be subpoenaed to testify at this hearing; it should take place ten days after the suspect is arrested.

10. If the municipal court judge decides there is enough evidence for a trial, the case may go to superior court.

11. The suspect is arraigned in superior court, or if he pleads guilty, the suspect is charged and sentenced.

12. A pre-trial hearing [is held]. (Your attendance is not necessary.)

13. Trial.

14. Acquittal or sentencing.[6]

Civil Suit

One last matter to address with regard to reporting a rape to the authorities is the victim's option to file a civil suit. The pace of criminal proceedings is often slow and may prove distressing to the victim and those close to her. As a result, if you are a victim, you may choose to file a civil suit before, during, or after the criminal proceedings. Unlike the criminal proceedings which require testimony and substantiating evidence showing the suspect to be guilty "beyond a reasonable doubt," the civil proceedings require only "a preponderance of evidence." You will have to retain your own attorney or go to small claims court.

Also, if you were assaulted in a public area, such as a parking lot or structure, you may be able to sue the owner(s) for negligence. You should discuss these matters with your attorney as well as with your pastor. God speaks clearly in Scripture about suing, and even in a case of rape, you will want to consider all aspects.

My own case has never gone to court. The rapist was disguised, fingerprints were impossible to lift, and there were no witnesses, so no suspect has been arrested. I am depending on God's promises of justice. Humanly speaking, it has been extremely frustrating, for as far as I know, my assailant is free. I don't know if I was his first victim, his tenth, or his fiftieth. But God does. I don't know if he has ever given that rape in January of 1979 another thought. But God does. I don't know if my pleas based on my Christian faith caused him to turn to Christ. But God does. It's been my prayer for nearly a decade that my assailant would be caught, arrested, imprisoned and sent through a treatment program for rehabilitation. But most of all, I pray that he's been through God's program of repentance.

"Never take your own revenge, beloved, but leave room for the wrath of God, for it is written, 'Vengeance is Mine, I will repay,' says the Lord" (Romans 12:19).

6

I Don't Know How to Tell You This. . .

L ate afternoon was bringing darkness now, and during the fifteen-minute ride back to the house, I wondered if Nick would be there when we arrived. My pounding heart ached as I thought about what lay ahead. *How do you tell your husband you have been raped?* Although unfounded, fears of condemnation swelled in my mind. *I can't do it! Lord, please,* I begged, *if there is any other way for Nick to find out, let it work out. I can't tell him. Please, spare me that agony.*

I could see my husband through the open kitchen window as we pulled up in front of the house. Jody parked across the street behind the police car, and Nick seemed to be straining to make out what was happening outside. *Does he see the police car? Lord, help,* I pleaded. *How will I get through these next moments?*

I got out of Jody's car and walked slowly around the back of it to cross the street. I dreaded every step, knowing each one brought me closer to relating my terrifying experience.

Suddenly Nick came running toward me through the open back gate. His long strides were easy for his six-foot-two, teddy-bear frame, and before I could catch my breath, he swooped me up in his outstretched arms, enveloping me in his embrace. I was stunned.

"Jen, oh, Jen. I love you. I love you so much. Honey, are you all right?" he said, showering me with kisses and holding me close.

Any moment I expected him to barrage me with questions like Why are you in Jody's car? How come a police car is following you? Where are the girls? But he didn't ask anything. Instead, he cupped my face in his big soft hands and told me over and over how much he loved me. At the same time he looked me over like a mother checking over her first-born for flaws.

I was limp. Emotionally depleted. Yet somehow I managed to say, "I love you, too." With those words came a release of the tentacle-like tension that had gripped my body fibers, and a flood of uncontrollable sobs followed.

We were both crying as we stood clinging to each other, tears dampening our clothes. To my surprise we had met in the middle of the street and were spotlighted in the brightness of the street light. Locked in mutual grief and despair, we had never felt closer.

After what seemed a very long time, we turned to go into the house. I didn't think I could go back in, but with Nick's arms gently supporting and guiding me, together we made our way up the back steps. Though I was strengthened momentarily, I felt an eerie presence still lingering in the air. We entered the kitchen area, and I found myself stumbling backward as if overcome by a repugnant odor. Nausea rumbled in my stomach. I struggled with each step as we proceeded, and flashes of the rape stabbed at my mind.

Jody and the police officers followed us into the dining area. I didn't move from Nick's side. *Is the rapist out there watching? Will he come back and kill me as he threatened?*

It was then Nick told me Dr. Cantwell had reached him by phone and was in the process of detailing the rape when we arrived. Shivers ran like spears up and down my spine as I thought how awful that must have been for him to hear. I was relieved to be spared that pain, but the thought of his mental suffering was heart-wrenching to me.

Whatever Nick's personal feelings were that day, he shielded me from them. Every few moments he kept assuring me everything would be all right, and he continued to show me compassion and care. That evening he made arrangements for the girls and me to fly to my parents' home and stay for a week since I was so afraid the rapist would come back.

Telling Family and Friends

Informing others of a sexual assault often presents a dilemma. In order for others to meet the victim's emotional and physical needs of support, they will have to know of her crisis. Yet when a woman tells someone else that she has been victimized by this heinous crime, she is faced with tremendous risks of rejection. What will his response be? How will he act? Will he be suspicious and condemning? Will he think she brought this upon herself? Will he wonder if she was dressed suggestively? These thoughts, along with fears of shame and misunderstanding, are valid deterrents to telling others.

Although family and close friends will want to know of her rape crisis, there are a number of reasons some victims choose not to tell. Fear of condemnation is one of the main reasons. Feelings of humiliation and embarrassment may cause the victim to remain silent. In some instances, it may be that an elderly parent's physical condition could not handle that kind of traumatizing news. The list goes on and on. Each reason is valid in the victim's eyes. As in reporting the rape, the decision to tell anyone else belongs to the victim alone. Her wishes need to be respected.

Another factor that may affect a victim's decision not to tell is the feeling that the crisis belongs to her and that she must attempt bravery in bearing it by herself. This is an unhealthy attitude. The fact is, the victim is not the only person affected. Like a rock thrown into a calm lake, rape creates ravaging ripples in the lives of the primary family, extended family and those with whom she comes in contact. Friends, co-workers, and even strangers, may be affected by it.

When others know the circumstances, they are better able to understand the different actions and emotional fluctuations that the victim will no doubt experience. Otherwise, it's possible these people will take her thermometer-like moods personally and pull away just when she needs them most.

Even the telling of what seems a tragedy can bring triumph as God uses the crisis to minister to and encourage others. If we choose not to share, we'll only miss God's blessings, but those around us will miss a glimpse of God and an opportunity for growth. Allowing oneself to be vulnerable is allowing God's sovereignty to reign.

Discerning God's Timing

After praying about whether I should talk about my rape, I decided to share only when the Lord led me to do so. I'd trust God to show me open doors for communicating my crisis. When I told this decision to my friend Jody, she supported my plan. I was depending on God to help me be sensitive to the Holy Spirit's leading and to give me words to say. I claimed Matthew 10:20 as God's word to me: "For it is not you who speak, but it is the Spirit of your Father who speaks in you".

A few months after the rape, Nick and I were having dinner at the home of our special friend, Cheryl. It proved to be a divine appointment. During the evening, Cheryl was sharing about her new-found relationship with Jesus Christ. A mutual friend, Joe, stopped by unexpectedly. After exchanging greetings, we got settled with a cup of hot coffee and Cheryl continued talking about the power of God.

Joe, a handsome, ruddy-complected, ex-Marine in his early thirties, had many questions about how God helps people with struggles and problems, and he was restless. He stood up, put his hands on his hips and with a perplexed look on his face he asked, "You mean to say, if a strange man broke into your home, put one arm around your neck and threatened your life with a knife at your throat, you believe some guy in the sky is going to come to your rescue?"

I froze. My face must have turned white as my thoughts raced back to my nightmare . . . and then to my decision to trust the Holy Spirit's leading. Though Joe's questions weren't directed at any one of us in particular, I knew it was I who had to answer. God wanted my obedience. Quietly I nodded, "Yes, Joe, that's exactly what we mean."

It was then I heard God's gentle voice and the prompting of the Holy Spirit as He opened the door for me to tell Joe of the faithfulness of my great God. I believed God would take care of the effect of my story. My part was to communicate God's grace.

God had planned this moment in both of our lives. In the stillness of Cheryl's living room, I began to tell how God promises never to leave or forsake His children. When we call upon Him for help, guidance or strength, or for whatever our need may be, He is right there, ready to answer. All we have to do is ask.

With a confident, strong voice, I told Joe that the scene he had just described was almost identical to a crisis I had been through recently and that God had met my need by supplying peace and safety. Ironically, it was the beginning of healing for me as I humbled myself in the sight of the Lord by sharing my story.

By the time I finished relating my experience, I was emotionally drained. The room was still. Joe sat on the end of the couch, with his head buried in his hands, and wept. I was deeply moved by his unrestrained emotion and his sensitivity to my words.

Joe was silent the remainder of the evening. Later, when we were saying our good-byes, I encouraged him to start reading his Bible and discover for himself God's provisions of protection. He told me he would begin the very next day.

Ord L. Morrow says that the reality of life is often shocking. But for the grace of God, there is no relief from trials that come our way. When life is lived with God, we can have confidence that difficulties, problems, hard places and defeated hopes all can be taken by Him and reshaped into something beautiful. "A life lived 'under God' is not lived under the circumstances. 'Under God' we are victors, not victims!"[1]

That night at Cheryl's, God clearly showed me the reward for waiting upon Him and His perfect timing. He had used my encounter with evil to bring good as promised in Romans 8:28, and as demonstrated in Genesis 50:20.

You too may experience situations when God moves in your heart to speak under the direction of His Holy Spirit. Confident of His prodding, you can step out in faith believing Him for the outcome. God did take charge of the outcome in Joe's life. Weeks later he told me that after that night, he kept his promise and began reading his Bible. God is still at work in Joe's life and I'm confident the touch of the Master's hand will bring positive results.

Who to Tell

Does every circle of friends have to be told? Although each victim will have to make this decision for herself, it isn't necessary to tell every person she knows or meets. Aside from those she chooses to tell, there undoubtedly will be those who hear of the rape from others who know. That cannot be controlled and should not be a cause for worry to the victim.

People whom the victim might want to tell include her immediate and extended family, close friends, her pastor, employer and close work associates. Telling acquaintances, strangers and others should only be done with discretion and with God's leading. The following points may be helpful when deciding who to tell.

1. Is this a trusted friend?
2. Has my relationship with this person matured and developed?
3. What is my purpose in telling?
4. Have I sought God's guidance?
5. How might I feel in the future once I've related my story?
6. Will my telling satisfy my need to talk, or will it demonstrate God's triumph over tragedy?

Telling Your Husband

One morning at the beauty shop when I was having my hair done, the discussion centered on rape. Tom, my beautician's husband, asserted, "If my wife were ever raped, I'd kill the bastard." We may cringe at the thought of such violence, but this is often the response. Not only has his wife been violated, but he, too, has been assaulted in a very real sense. His image as protector and his masculinity have been marred. In many cases this is a threat to a man's ego.

Recently my friend, Fred Littauer, sent me an article from a Southern California newspaper. The article was entitled, "A Case of Rape: Advice for the Husbands of Victims."[2] It told about a young woman named Lisa who was raped while her husband Barry was out of town. Barry did all the wrong things. He told Lisa he wanted to kill the rapist and asked for a description of her attacker. When Lisa was unable to provide the description, he accused her of being uncooperative. As time went on Barry continued talking about the rape, implying that Lisa was responsible. He started drinking heavily, ignored their young son, and demanded sexual attention before Lisa was emotionally ready to respond.

The significant others in a victim's life play a crucial role in her recovery. Their actions and attitudes will help or hinder her return to normalcy. A husband's support of his victimized wife helps him come to terms with his own emotions. In the book, *If She Is Raped: A Book for Husbands, Fathers, and Male Friends,* author Alan McEvoy also writes about the unsupportive partner whose anger and distrust blind him to the victim's feelings and the problems she faces.[3]

A husband's lack of support significantly hinders his wife's steps to recovery, increases her distress, and lengthens the recovery period. The following suggestions may be helpful if you ever should have to tell your husband you were raped:

1. If possible, take time to plan what will be said.
2. You may want to have a close friend, family member or pastor present.
3. You should tell yourself repeatedly, *I am not responsible for what happened to me.*

4. Pray for inner strength to withstand negative or violent reactions.
5. Should there be an explosive response, remember that the anger is directed at what has happened, not at you.
6. Ask for time, distance, quiet, music, a walk, or whatever *you* need during this time when you are fragile.

Telling Your Children

On the day of my rape it was obvious that something drastic had happened to me physically. My children had to be given some kind of explanation. But my agony over the assault convinced me I couldn't cope with telling them their mother had been raped. I had suffered with chronic illness for nearly five years prior to the attack, so I let them think my crisis was a continuation of past problems. While that made it easier for me, it made them afraid they might lose someone who gave them much of their safety and security. I wanted to shelter them from the truth, so I let them believe a lie.

Over the years that lie nearly destroyed me. The energy expended protecting them from the truth caused increasing stress. One day, about two and a half years later, I exploded in a violent rage.

As a result of that, I made an appointment with a counselor at church and asked him if I should tell the girls about my rape. To my surprise, he didn't answer yes or no, and I discovered I was to look to God for the guidance I needed. I also needed to trust myself. Since I'd never learned to trust myself, I would really have to trust God.

One afternoon when Nicole was twelve and Lisa was eleven, the three of us were home alone, and God placed the burden upon my heart that this was the day to talk with them. I called the girls into the den where it was cozy and comfortable. We sat on scattered pillows on the floor.

"Girls, I have something I want to talk to you about," I softly said.

Nicole asked, "What is it, Mom?"

"Is something wrong with Dad?" Lisa asked.

"No," I answered. "Do you remember the afternoon a few years ago when I was real sick and Carol took all of us to Dr. Cantwell's office?" I knew this was a crucial moment and I silently prayed for the Lord to give me the right words.

"I'll never forget it. We were so scared you were going to die, Mom. We were really scared," Nicole said.

"Yeah, Mom, what about it? It was your kidney problem, wasn't it? You told us you had to get to the doctor right away," Lisa added.

"Yes, girls, that's what I said. I want to tell you a little more about that afternoon. You see, while you were at school and Amy was sleeping, a strange man came into our house and hurt Mommy. He frightened me, and that's why we had to get out of the house, and why the next day we went to stay with Grandma for awhile," I quietly said.

"Mom, why do you have tears in your eyes? What's wrong?" Nicole asked.

"You see, honey," I answered, "this man raped me. That's why I have been so scared at times and have acted in strange ways you didn't understand. I have felt very afraid when things were out of my control or when strangers were around."

Nicole started crying, and she got up and hugged me. "I'm so glad you're here now," she said.

"Where else would I be?"

"Dead," she boomed, relieved to see I was O.K.

I told her I was glad I was here, too, and then we all embraced and kissed. Lisa sat close to me and we talked for two hours about trusting Jesus in times of trouble.

I concluded our time of sharing by telling them why I get so excited about life. I believed God had restored my health and had given me a second chance at life. I told them of a promise I made to the Lord the day of the rape. I had vowed that, if I lived through it, I would no longer hide my Christianity. I promised to let my light shine and to serve God. With His help I would make an impact in others' lives for Him. "He's a pretty great God," I said, and they readily agreed.

Now Nicole and Lisa are teens, and as they matured through the years, they requested more information. We have maintained on-going, open communication about my rape and at times they have used my story to minister to hurting friends at school or church.

Due to circumstances beyond my control, telling Amy came sooner than I wanted. From my perspective, it wasn't God's timing. But even so, God was guiding when I sat Amy down one morning and briefly explained what had happened. She was only eight years old, and it was a very sensitive but special time. As she has grown and asked more questions, I have given her short and simple answers without belaboring my trauma.

Before telling a child about a rape, one should consider the age of the child, his or her level of emotional maturity, and the availability of support (counselors, aunts and uncles, church family, teachers, etc.).

Children under eight can be told that "a man hurt Mommy but she is O.K. now. She is going to be all right." If they ask questions, answer them as simply as possible without going into detail. It's best not to speak of weapons used or other forms of violence. Use phrases they understand. Nine- to twelve-year-olds will likely have more questions and won't settle for evasive answers. They may ask what the rapist looked like, if you knew him, what he did, and other pointed questions.

Whether the children are told of the rape or not, they will sense something is wrong. Whatever their age, they will be aware of a family crisis. It is best for you to acknowledge you are in crisis, but you can reassure them by telling them you will get help. Ignoring or downplaying what is obvious to the children can set the stage for greater problems. Lack of validation of their fearful feelings undermines the children's self-trust, and that can hinder their emotional growth and the development of their self-confidence.

It also should be explained to the children that the man who hurt Mommy is sick and needs help. Telling them that you may act differently for a while and that you aren't angry with them but very upset about what happened may give them more security. They should be encouraged to talk with you just like they always have, to send you notes or letters, give you lots of hugs, and ask God to help you feel better.[4]

Telling a Teenager

When the rape victim is a mother with teens, it's important to distinguish between conjugal love and sexual violence as she explains the rape. For teenagers today, the influx of video presentations and musical lyrics blared over radios often depicts intercourse as glamorized violence. Rape is not glamorous. Rape is violent. It is a crime and needs to be addressed aggressively to the teenager. Teens should be encouraged to give their love and support to their mother. They need to understand that healing will take time. They can be assured that with their acceptance and patience, their mother will return to her normal self. There is hope for her recovery.

Rape is a caustic word. No one likes to think or talk about it. It's often unpleasant for us to listen to a victim who desperately needs a caring friend with an open ear. If we are to fulfill God's greatest commandment of loving one another, we must be willing to make the time to hear and respond with His love. Rape victims don't know how to tell us about their tragedy, but if we let the Lord minister through us, the healing process will be speeded up in their lives.

__ 7 _____

"Nice Girls Don't Get Raped"

When the attack becomes known, rape victims inevitably will encounter different reactions. Some people will be supportive and some will react negatively, but the most destructive reaction is the one that implies guilt on the part of the victim. The one that places the responsibility of the rape, of this horrible violent crime, on the innocent victim. The one that says, "If you had been a nice girl, a good girl, this wouldn't have happened to you."

Prior to my rape I, like many other people, had my ideas of what type of woman was raped. She definitely was not of the same moral standard as I and surely frequented places I didn't. But about eight months after the rape a trusted friend gave me her view as we were leaving a morning Bible study. "Well," she said, even though she knew about my experience, "I would never allow myself to be in a vulnerable situation that might lead to rape. If a woman is raped, she must have asked for it. Certainly that could never happen to a decent woman." I had to struggle to maintain my dignity, and can only believe that she did not realize the impact her words would have on me.

One of the most common popular beliefs, even today, is that "only 'loose' women get raped; nice girls don't get raped."

So writes Shirley Gardiner in *A Book About Sexual Assault*.[1]
Therefore, much of the trauma experienced by the victim
evolves from the self-doubt and guilt engendered by these
beliefs. She wonders, *Could I have prevented it? Did I bring
it on myself?*

Paradoxically, when a woman becomes a victim of this
violent crime, it's up to her to prove her own innocence.
Some people believe, and sometimes so does the victim
herself, that the only sure way she can prove her virtue is to
risk death resisting her attacker.

At one time, I foolishly believed that if I conformed to
social definitions of "nice girl" behavior, that, along with my
Christian background, would protect me from the danger of
sexual assault. The fact is that every woman, regardless of
economic background, age, physical appearance, geographic
location or social position, is vulnerable. She needs to take
responsibility for herself to be informed and aware.

Girls who obey their mothers, girls who remain virgins
until marriage, girls who avoid bars, girls who are polite and
mannerly, girls who are kind to the elderly, girls who help
others, girls who sing in church choirs, girls who are devoted
to family, girls who are socially prominent, and girls who are
"good girls" do get raped.

In the September 5, 1983, issue of *Time* magazine,
Maureen Dowd wrote about a pastor's daughter who was gang
raped by nine Ohio State athletes. She never returned to school.[2]

In another case, in New Bedford, Massachusetts, a young
woman in a bar was hoisted up onto a table and raped. Some
may consider her a "loose" woman for being in the bar in
the first place, but who is to say if she was any more "loose"
than a nurse leaving hospital duty late at night? If the nurse
were raped, certainly it would not be implied that she invited
the assault by her "loose" behavior. But the feelings are nearly
unanimous that the woman in the bar was not a "nice" girl
and, therefore, deserved to be raped.

Furthermore, when a woman is raped the definition of
her virtue frequently changes. The sexual assault now credits
her with loose morality — "She must be 'loose' if she was
raped."

One rape victim, a former drug addict, left the scene of the rape and went directly to a nearby police station. She was convinced her prompt action would lead to the arrest of the rapist. Though she was cut and bruised and gave a clear description of the rapist and his car, when the police noticed the traces of her former addiction, they stopped filing the report. They sympathetically suggested it was useless to pursue the case. She would have no credibility in court. Her former addiction would define her as "loose" and therefore "deserving" of rape.

Unfortunately, these factors affect the reporting of rape. Unless she has been brutally beaten and battered by the stereotypic psychopathic rapist, or unless she can prove she was a virgin (or a monogamously married woman of known respectability), reporting will result in assaults on her character. Many women, aware of these possible repercussions and injustices, simply choose not to report a rape.

At times when I have talked about being a rape victim, I was completely unaware of a degree of preconceived guilt on my part. Others would blame me, and though I would get defensive verbally, inside I became confused and really doubted my innocence. After awhile I realized that I couldn't fight a battle of conflict and confusion like that, but God could, and I eventually allowed Him to take it over and give me the victory. If you are the victim, the important thing for you to do is to focus on the fact that you *are* a *victim* of a violent crime. The perpetrator, not the victim, is punishable with a prison sentence.

Although that is an undeniable truth, a rape victim still may be harassed, ostracized, even ridiculed, and the label may remain with her throughout her life. In Canada and the United States, it is not uncommon for a known victim to receive anonymous phone calls suggesting sexual encounters. I, along with many other victims, have received such distressing calls. All such abuse becomes a stumbling block to the victim who is struggling for recovery.

At these times we can take a strong position in the sanctity of God's promises. He will arm us to stand firm against the schemes of the devil.

Common Reactions

The thought of being raped brings different images to mind for every woman. Some may speculate as to how they would feel or what they would do if raped. Others tend to focus on the sexual aspect of the assault. But according to *Survivor*, "Rape crisis counselors have found most victims experience sexual assault as a severe emotional and physical violation."[3]

Dr. Nicholas Growth, director of an innovative sex-offender rehabilitation program at the state prison in Somers, Connecticut, writes, "Rape is the sexual expression of aggression."[4] Only when that fact is believed will the focus on the victim's character end. Then, when the raped woman is rightly viewed as the victim of a violent crime, those around her can compassionately offer their counsel.

Emotional Stages of Reaction

Since each woman is specially designed by God, no two women have the same reaction to rape. But the majority of victims *tend* to react similarly, in three stages.

Stage one: This is described by Gail Abarbanel:

> In initial contacts with rape victims, the most significant impacts of rape trauma may be "invisible." Victims seen soon after the assault may appear deceptively calm. They experience numbness, shock and disbelief. They appear dazed, subdued and contained. They may find it difficult to concentrate or make decisions; thus, they appear unsure, confused and distracted. They have flashbacks in which they relive parts of the assault and their loss of control. Thus, they seem preoccupied. Victims also have a strong need to deny and block out the experience and the feelings it produces. They may, therefore, engage in routine conversation or resist talking about the assault. These defenses are adaptive and protective. By postponing the feelings, the victim gives herself time to prepare for them. This presentation of a seemingly calm demeanor immediately following the rape, though characteristic of rape trauma, contradicts the expectations most people have about

rape victims. This is, however, a normal and usual response to the overwhelming nature of the assault experience.[5]

Stage two: The second stage of emotional reaction begins about a week after the rape. It is a period of outward adjustment in which the victim wants to erase the rape from her memory and continue with her life in a normal manner. She may even deny expressed feelings of the previous week. Although this approach is self-protective and rational, remaining in this stage is unhealthy. If she continues to suppress her true emotions, she does not give herself the opportunity to "finish" the experience and recover.[6] The sad part is that first she was robbed by the rapist, and now she robs herself, denying herself the opportunity of reaching her full potential and living a productive life.

Stage three: In this stage, which may begin a few weeks or many years after the rape, the victim has a need to express her feelings about herself — her anger, her guilt, her depression and her confusion (rape trauma syndrome). She may be unable to stop thinking about it, becoming preoccupied with the assault and the assailant.[7] As a result, she may feel she is going crazy. This is the time for the victim to seek professional help through counseling and psychotherapy. She needs to talk. Studies show that it takes from six months to six years for most victims to feel normal again. For others, the process of healing can continue throughout their lives.

Rape Trauma Syndrome

Rape trauma syndrome is the term used to identify the combination of physical, emotional and psychological reactions to rape. Listed below are examples of reactions typical of rape victims. Not every victim will experience every reaction, but at least a few of these symptoms are to be expected and are normal whenever they occur. If you are the victim, you can expect to feel some of these things as the direct result of the rapist's violation of your safety, control, autonomy and self-esteem. Whatever you experience, remember that your feelings are neither right nor wrong. They are just feelings.

One example is the common feeling of guilt. It is a normal feeling, experienced by many rape victims, but it has no basis. This list will give you an idea of what the majority of rape victims feel at some time during their stages of recovery.

Preoccupation with the need for survival.

Humiliation, degradation, embarrassment, shame, guilt, self-blame.

Powerlessness, vulnerability, helplessness.

Anger, desire for revenge.

Suspicion and fright of others.

Fear of physical injury or death.

Lack of stability, sudden changes of mood.

Irritation with others close to you.

Need for denying that it even occurred.

Hypersensitivity.

Fear of crowds.

Fear of being alone or entering your home alone.

Fear of men.

Fear of sex or diminished sex drive (or the reverse).

Need for more physical affection.

Flashbacks focused on moment of loss of control (rather than on moment of penetration).

Repulsion of characteristics unique to the rapist (examples: mustache, the particular scent of his cologne, alcohol).

Need for knowing why it happened (a way of regaining control and convincing yourself that you can prevent it from happening again).

A loathing for your body.[8]

According to *Survivor,* the following are also examples of typical reactions to sexual assault.

Emotional shock: I feel so numb.

Disbelief: Did it really happen? Why me?

Embarrassment: What will people think? No, I can't tell my family.

Shame: I feel so dirty, like there is something wrong with me now. I want to wash my hands all day long.

Guilt: I feel as if I did something to make this happen to me. If only I had. . .

Depression: How am I going to go on? I feel so tired and hopeless.

Powerlessness: Will I ever feel in control again?

Disorientation: I can't sit still. I'm having trouble getting through the day. I'm just overwhelmed!

Re-triggering: I keep having flashbacks. I wish they would stop.

Denial: Wasn't it "just" a rape?

Fear: I'm afraid of so many things. Will I get pregnant or get [a venereal disease]? Am I safe? Can people tell what's happened to me? Will I ever want to be intimate again? Will I ever get over this? I'm afraid I'm going crazy. I have nightmares that terrify me.

Anxiety: I'm a nervous wreck! I have trouble breathing. (Anxiety often is expressed in physical symptoms, like difficulty breathing or muscle tension, sleep disturbances, change in eating habits, nausea, stomach problems, nightmares, bed-wetting.)

Anger: I want to kill him![9]

Negative Comments and Positive Reactions

Negative comments from insensitive or uninformed people can be devastating to the rape victim. "Why didn't you go into the house when you heard the dog barking?" was one such comment I struggled over. Since I already felt guilty and responsible, I wondered the same thing, yet felt defensive toward such questions. The fact was our little dog, Trixie, barked at everything — falling leaves, people passing, stray cats, the mail man, anything. Although on the day of the rape I heard her barking, I was deep in thought and intent on finishing my planting project. Regardless, I was not responsible for the rape, and neither is any other rape victim.

Remembering that she is not responsible for her rape can free the victim from being defensive. She can trust God's grace to intervene, and she can minister by her gentle yet honest response. It will help for her to think of her knowledgeable response as a step toward furthering rape education for the other person, and it also will decrease criticism of her

character. At times this will be difficult, but it is possible
when harnessed by the Holy Spirit.

Paula, in her early forties, was raped in a large hotel in
Southern California. A knife was used to threaten her and she
was cut many times in the struggle. A long-time friend learned
of the assault and stormed, "Why didn't you scream?" Paula
had been in a state of "frozen fright," a form of shock as
mentioned in chapter 5. She was immobilized by fear and
incapable of resisting or screaming. She finally began to
understand through counseling why she was unable to scream,
and then was able to contribute to the education of those who
wondered.

It can also be helpful to understand that caustic comments
usually stem from other people's insecurity, their fear of rape
and their desire to protect themselves from emotional pain.
They begin to realize that if this could happen to someone
they know, then it could happen to them, and that's a thought
they most likely will not want to face.

The Seduction of Satan

Satan, our enemy, is constantly on the prowl seeking
someone to devour. A rape victim is vulnerable and may not
be on guard against the schemes of the devil. She may be
unstable in her mind and, therefore, an easy prey. She needs
to depend on God's strength as a shield protecting her from
disturbing comments. For those accusing statements that slip
through, God's grace will supply simple responses to be given
in love. It is in keeping with God's unfathomable ways that
now in her weakness God will use her to minister His love
to others.

For a victim who already feels guilty and carries the
responsibility for her rape, these steps of faith will be challeng-
ing. If she chooses to accept the challenge, I'm confident she
will grow emotionally and spiritually as God gives her grace.

In the spring of 1980, nearly a year and a half after my
assault, Marilyn (the friend I had tried to contact) called to
say she'd found a letter she had composed one week after
the rape. It was written to me and meant to encourage and

support me, but she had misplaced it. Now she was going to send it through the mail. It was especially meaningful because what she had said would happen if I'd trust God had already begun happening.

Dearest Jennifer,
First of all I want you to know that my love and prayers go out to you in this, your time of need. I want you to know that God has permitted you to be in a very unique position. This is surely a time of trial for you, but God is faithful and will not permit you to be tempted above what you are able to stand. Please don't forget the wonderful joy and blessing you had before this experience befell you.

I really believe that you are going to be used in a very special way. I know you are confused, angry and hurt, but realize that your precious Lord Jesus is right there with you and can heal your deepest wounds. Your relationship with Him now is the most important thing. You had told me that you thought God was going to use you and so He is. He is going to do a healing work in you so that you may be a witness of His power and might.

Please don't despair. Praise God and let His precious Holy Spirit heal you through and through. You are a very precious person and loved by your Lord. He is going to give you a witness and a closer relationship with Him that will outshadow anything you have gone through.

I thank God for your sweet spirit and witness. He will be victorious through you. If I can ever help or be of any assistance, please feel free to call on me. You are where God can give you His might and love, and surely He will. Please, God, bless and wash away every fear and doubt. To God be the *victory!* Great things He has done!

Love in Christ,
Marilyn

8

Lost and All Alone

On the afternoon of my rape I had screamed, cried, and pleaded to be left alone by the rapist. Then I remembered that Nick *had* left me alone. I reasoned that if he had stayed with me on his day off instead of playing golf, this wouldn't have happened to me. My neighbors had left me alone — they weren't home; the girls were gone; no family members were close by who could drop in; and my friends were all busy. I was totally alone. Even God had left me alone. How else could this evil have penetrated God's walls of protection around me? *Why, God? Why have You forsaken me? What have I done wrong? What sin have I committed? I am Your faithful servant. I love You. I've begun to witness for You in the marketplace. I'd give my life for You. But, God, where are You? I can't see You. I can't hear You. I don't feel Your presence.*

Standing on the edge of a wilderness I was lost. At least Moses had a staff to hold. I had nothing. Whatever I tried to grip slipped away, and I was left alone again.

For the first weeks and months after the rape, I was intent on keeping my assault secret. Thoughts of condemnation and further humiliation made me fearful. In our conservative church family I had never heard of anyone being raped. What if those people had preconceived ideas about rape victims? How could I speak up and risk rejection? I didn't have the strength to be stoical, and therefore continued in my suffering, still alone.

During the next few years I sank deeper and deeper into an inner depression as I wandered in my wilderness with no sight of the promised land. Yet on the outside, my happy appearance and smiling face spoke of recovery. I managed to wear a facade successfully for almost three and a half years, but I was obsessed with discovering *why* I had been raped. Surprisingly, I never doubted God would work it for my good, but I still had to find out why I had been victimized in this way.

There are many rape victims who have never told anyone. They wander aimlessly in their own private wilderness waiting to be rescued and relieved from their plight. Yet, the key to escape lies in expressing the pain to those who can put aside their assumptions and extend their love and support.

In God's perfect timing, He lifted me out of my bog and mire and set me on firmer ground. He knew my pain and fear. He allowed situations to rise that would cause me to grow closer to Him as I struggled for answers.

About two years after the rape, I had breakfast with my friend Donna Jean Wood and her husband George. After sharing my experience with them I asked them to remember me in prayer. The following week I received a greeting card with a picture on the front of a beautiful green valley with snow-capped mountains in the background. The sun was setting and in one corner was a rainbow. Evergreen trees dotted the hills that rose above a rushing river. Along the embankment were wild flowers and a butterfly. An eagle soared above the peaks.

The card was from Donna. Below her signature she had jotted a verse:

> Do not call to mind the former things, or ponder things of the past. Behold, I will do something new, now it will spring forth; will you not be aware of it? I will even make a roadway in the wilderness, rivers in the desert (Isaiah 43:18,19).

That card and verse have become a symbol and an expression of what God has done for me and of His sustaining power when I have felt forgotten and alone.

God had not abandoned me as I sometimes thought. He did make a roadway in my wilderness, and He guided me to the river when I was in the desert of depression. He now lights the path for me to drink continually from living waters. As I continue to seek His path, He assures me I will never thirst again.

If you are in that wilderness like I once was, it is my prayer for you that God will send you caring friends as He sent George and Donna Jean to me. Chances are they have already crossed your path, but you may be holding back. Step out in faith, for the rejoicing in the Lord that will surely come is worth the risk. I'm praying for God's sustaining strength for you.

Reactions of Family and Friends

As mentioned in chapter 7, most women react to rape with shock and disbelief. Though the victim is the one primarily affected, family and friends are affected also. Both play vital parts in her recovery.

Studies show that the degree of support received from the victim's family directly influences her rate of recovery. Family reactions can range from being empathic to enraged, covering a vast array of both positive and negative feelings. Although outwardly accepting, secretly they may be suspicious of the rape victim. While she is reacting to the fear and terror of the crime, the family may be reacting to the sexual aspects.

People frequently avoid rape victims, much like they avoid families in grief following a death of one of their members. It is not because they do not care but because they don't know what to say. Lauren Littauer Briggs has written a book entitled *What You Can Say. . . When You Don't Know What to Say,* which offers suggestions to those who grope for ways to express their sympathy. As with the death of a loved one, a victim often experiences a time of grief and mourning. In a very real sense, she has experienced a living death of her spirit, and she needs to work through the process of mourning her loss before she can become whole and complete in her healing.

There will be times when you, as a family member or friend, will feel overwhelmed and tired of hearing about your loved one's rape. At these times it's tempting to blame her for so many interruptions in your life. But remember, she did not do this to you. She was forced against her will to participate in a crime, and she doesn't want to deal with it any more than you do.

Sometimes it's important to remind family members who the true victim is. For example, in *Sexual Violence: The Unmentionable Sin,* Marie Fortune writes, "The mother of a fourteen-year-old rape victim said to a minister, 'I can't believe this happened to me.' The minister replied, 'It didn't happen to you. It happened to your daughter and she needs you to support her now.' "[1] This does not mean we should deny the impact on family members, but we must realize the crisis belongs to the victim. When other family members take on the crisis as their own, the victim too often feels a responsibility to stop and take care of them. Thus, her recovery process is suspended for a time. A minister or professional counselor can be helpful in dealing with the family members' feelings, apart from the victim, so that they too receive effective support.

Note to Family and Friends

Be supportive and uncritical.

As mentioned before, some victims try to keep the rape entirely to themselves, wanting to hide it even from family and friends until they feel they are back in control. Their motive is frequently self-protection, but they actually are living with self-disillusion and even are inviting more pain.

Although talking about the rape before the victim is ready could be harmful, you can encourage her to talk about her feelings. You should listen nonjudgmentally and be patient when she needs to ventilate, repeating the same story over and over. It's best not to tell her to forget about it and go on with her life. The time for her to do that will come eventually, but right after the rape it is not possible. She couldn't forget if she tried.

If she rambles about other things, let her. The change of subject will give her a mental rest. Also, allow her the freedom to talk with whomever she wants and avoid forcing her to talk with you or some other person of your choosing, but let her know she can depend on you and that you are available anytime, day or night. (For many victims, nights are the hardest to endure.) Validate her feelings and let her know you are praying for her needs.

Treat the victim with dignity. Ask how she feels, what's bothering her, and how you can help. Do this gently without probing. If she doesn't answer, let her know that's O.K.

Avoid being overprotective, and be honest about your own feelings concerning her rape and the rapist. But do not assume you know what she is thinking and feeling. When you ask questions, give her time to answer. Encourage her to seek counseling. Offer to go with her if she needs that support, yet be willing for her to go alone if she chooses.

Forgiving the Rapist

Although I forgave the rapist intellectually in the first few months after my assault, it was many years before I forgave him in my heart. Difficult, you say? I say, without the working of the Holy Spirit, impossible.

The Bible clearly instructs us to forgive anyone who has hurt us physically or emotionally. Lewis B. Smedes writes in *Forgive and Forget: Healing the Hurts We Don't Deserve,* "If you cannot free people from their wrongs and see them as the needy people they are, you enslave yourself to your own painful past, and by fastening yourself to the past, you let your hate become your future. You can reverse your future only by releasing other people from their pasts." Smedes goes on to say, "You will know that forgiveness has begun when you recall those who hurt you and feel the power to wish them well."[2]

Since, to my knowledge, my rapist was never caught, there is a certain lack of closure about that pain in my life.

Though I have forgiven him and do wish him wholeness through salvation, loose ends remain. But recently God prompted one convicted rapist, Paul, who is serving a prison sentence, to write to me after seeing me on a nationwide TV interview. I agonized for four months before I could answer him. Now we have been corresponding and God is working in both of our lives.

Paul requested a copy of my testimony which had been published in *Seek*.[3] In that article, my pain is depicted on the left side of the page and the pain of the mother-in-law and of the wife of a convicted rapist on the right side. Paul has passed the article to other inmates and has sent a copy to his ex-wife. Since then, he has sent me his testimony. He is a bruised and battered man who has cried out to God to forgive him of the crimes he committed. Now he attends a prison Bible study, is enrolled in a Christian college and seminary and has a burden for other men who suffer in the way he once did.

The Day I Grew Up

From as far back as I can remember I'd always been a fearful child. I was very sensitive and easily frightened, a perfect target for practical jokers. I was plagued for many years with a fear of noises, of shadows and of the dark. Jumpy by nature, I had a reputation as an easy prey for pranksters and couldn't seem to shake this image. Not only was I victimized by classmates, but I frequently felt violated by my own family and frustrated that they didn't take my feelings and fears seriously. At times I felt humiliated and couldn't understand why no one came to my defense.

When my brother and I were children, an uncle took us for a ride in his 1932 shiny black Model-A Ford. At first it was fun, but when he told us he was going to jump the river where the bridge was washed out, I became hysterical. Everyone else roared with laughter at my screams of panic. None of us realized the psychological impact these traumas would have on my later life.

As a grown woman, I was embarrassed by these outward

tendencies, but inside I was panic-struck. I began working for Dr. Cantwell at the age of twenty-three. I can remember standing in the instrument room deep in thought and unaware that Dr. Cantwell had entered through the back door. When he said, "Good morning," I'd drop the instruments, fling myself around and scream.

Ten years later, I stood in my back yard repotting plants. I had a distinct feeling I was being watched, but rather than panic with hysteria as I had in the past, ironically I decided this was the day I would grow up. Hadn't I been a scaredy-cat long enough? That very day I chose to overcome my childish ways, and I stood my ground. I was no longer going to be shackled by fear and made to feel like a fool.

I suffered a lack of self-trust though, and I didn't acknowledge my body's warning, my gut feeling that said I was being watched. I assumed it was my skittish past and I surely wasn't going to go on playing the old mental tapes based on immaturity, insecurity and an overactive imagination!

Since that day, the day my rape occurred, God has been faithful in showing me He will supply inner strength enabling me to trust myself when circumstances threaten to control my life. Now, by depending upon His provision in times of trial, I can be confident He will work the outcome for my good, even when waters are troubled.

Depending on God

A little over a year after the rape, a stressful situation arose, and this time I acted with strength and conviction. One morning when Nicole and Lisa were home sick from school, Amy and I went out to wash the car. It was the first time I'd ventured out of the house on my own, and though I was nervous, I depended on God's sustaining safety while completing the task.

Amy was close by washing her tricycle while I was hosing off the soap from the car. About a block away an older-looking man in faded gray-blue, disheveled clothes appeared to be wandering toward us down the middle of the street.

What is this man doing? Why is he weaving like that? Oh . . . Oh, no. He's coming toward Amy and me.

"Amy," I yelled, without thinking. "Drop the hose and come here, *now.* We are going in the house for a minute." She looked at me perplexed. I could tell she was questioning why in the world we should go into the house when she was having so much fun.

Grabbing her, I carried her inside the yard and looked back to see where the man had gone and what he was doing. Something seemed odd about him, but I couldn't figure out what it was. Although he was still weaving as he walked, he managed to cross over to our side of the street. We were shielded from his view by the ivy that covered a portion of the chain link fence around our corner house, but soon his position would make us clearly visible.

Putting Amy down, I closed the gate. She wandered out into the middle of the back yard. *No, Amy, we're not playing hide-and-seek now.* Frantic, I called for her to come. I was afraid running to get her would draw the man's attention our way. Because of his drug-crazed look, I couldn't take that risk.

By this time, Nicole and Lisa had come to the back door to see what the commotion was about. It seemed they were always with me when absurd situations happened, and now they were asking, "Mom, what's the matter?"

"Oh, nothing, honey," I answered. "We just wanted to come in because some weird man is walking down the middle of the street, and I thought we would stay in the house until he passed. You girls go back and lie down while I get Amy in here."

Fear ran rampant through my body. I decided to call the police. I wasn't about to wait and see what this man's intentions were. I thought he was crazy, on drugs, or just drunk, but I knew something was very strange. After getting Amy into the house, I slipped into the bedroom and dialed the now memorized police number.

The police officer asked what the man was doing.

"Doing? Well, nothing specifically," I answered. "But he looks real strange and . . . like a werewolf. I just know something is wrong. He's weaving all over the street."

"A what, lady? Did you say he looks like a werewolf?" the officer asked.   "Well . . . you know, he reminds me of that man who played the werewolf in the old movie. It's the shape of his head and the way he's sort of staggering."

"O.K., Ma'am. We'll send out a patrol to check on this man. In the meantime, stay in your house and keep the doors locked," continued the officer.

I stayed in the bedroom for fifteen minutes peering out through the curtain. When I came out, the girls surrounded me and told me there was a policeman on a motorcycle at our back gate. I told them I had called the police to check out this strange man. He didn't seem to come from our neighborhood.

"You did what?" Lisa roared. "Oh, Mom, that's dumb. He's just walking down the street minding his own business."

"Yes, dear, but something just isn't right. Since we are here alone I thought it best to let the police handle it. If it's nothing, well, nothing's lost. But if he's dangerous or something, the police should know about him."

By now the man had passed our house and was out of sight. I felt absurd. *What's the matter with me? Am I some hysterical lady reacting to a poor, harmless, old man?* I called the police again and told them they might as well radio the officer at our back gate and cancel the call. They said they would continue checking out the man to make sure everything was O.K. Since I'd not yet told the girls about the rape, they thought I'd gone off the deep end. By now, I was questioning my actions, too.

After I gave the officer at our gate a description of the man, he rode off to investigate. About forty minutes later, the policeman came back. I went to the gate, curious about what had happened.

"Ma'am, I just want to tell you it was a good thing you had the sense to call," the officer said. "We arrested the man down at the corner. He had attacked a lady in her car as she was stopped at the stop sign. He was beating her and she lay slumped in the seat, nearly unconscious. She could have been killed if it hadn't been for your call. Thanks, Ma'am, you sure did the right thing. He's a very violent man."

"Oh, well . . . uh. . . You're welcome. I'm glad I called, too. I had the strongest feeling about him, but I couldn't figure it out," I said, shocked by the brutal reality of his comments.

"Girls, girls," I called as I went into the house. "I want to talk with you." After I told them how the police caught the man, they felt proud of me and began jumping up and down. Suddenly, instead of being a nut, I became a heroine in their eyes.

That afternoon God showed me the value of being sensitive to the Holy Spirit's leading even when I didn't understand. In the past, I had regarded my intuitions and perceptions as illogical. Now God showed me His gift of spiritual discernment on which I could depend.

Recently, a young woman named Debra attended my "How to Stop Being a Victim" class. She told of suspicious feelings she once had. "I was on my way into the library and I saw these two fellows hanging around the trash bins, eyeing a car that was parked nearby. I had a queer feeling they were up to no good, but had no real reason to feel this way. When I came out of the library two hours later, the police were swarming in the parking lot and the car was gone."

Debra had ignored her feeling that something was wrong. She felt foolish about contacting the authorities because no laws had been broken. Had she trusted her internal signals and called the police, the outcome might have been different.

What if we act, then find our feelings were wrong? Maybe we misjudged our internal signal as the prompting of the Holy Spirit. We need not be embarrassed or feel foolish for having tried preventive measures. It can be life-saving. As we continue depending on God, we'll grow more sensitive to the Holy Spirit's prompting, distinguishing between spiritual discernment and unfounded anxiety.

9

Definition of Rape

Many women and men historically have had distorted ideas about what rape is and what it isn't. When they heard the word *rape,* or they learned that someone they knew was raped, they automatically assumed the rapist was perverted, an outcast of society, and they often felt that the victim somehow contributed to her fate.

The fact is today many people still have a narrow view about rape. Even in our enlightened times of increased awareness, spouses, family and friends of a victim tend to focus on rape as a sexual act rather than what it actually is: the sexual expression of aggression, as described by Dr. Nicholas Growth in his studies (see chapter 7).

In order to remove the stigma from rape victims, we must replace the old belief that rape is an offense motivated by desire for the attractive woman. Although the falsehood of this myth is adequately substantiated by experts, some people are not convinced that rape is a violent crime, a hostile act, and an attempt to hurt and humiliate. A band of robbers holding up a store uses guns, sticks or other weapons; a rapist assaulting a woman uses his penis as the weapon.

One counselor describes rape in this way: "Rape is the logical consequence of the way men and women are taught to treat each other. Boys learn at an early age that aggression and violence prove virility and masculinity, while girls learn to play hard-to-get."

The founder of the Center for Rape Concern in Philadelphia says this behavior perpetuates a "rape society."

Although legal definitions vary from state to state, the most comprehensive one says rape is the forced penetration of the vagina, mouth or anus by the penis, or any other object, against the will of the victim. Lesser violations are dealt with as assault and battery.

Sex offenses generally fall into one of these five categories:

1. Rape or assault with intent to rape
2. Child molestation
3. Exhibitionism and voyeurism
4. Incest
5. Miscellaneous offense (breaking and entering, arson, etc., in cases where there is sexual motivation).[1]

Helen Benedict defines rape in her book, *Recovery,* as any sexual act that is forced upon you.[2] In California, any form of sexual conduct carried out against a person's will is a crime, whether the person is male or female.

Section 26 of the basic California Penal Code gives us the following information about sexual assault:

The crime of rape is defined as an act of sexual intercourse, accomplished with a person not the spouse of the perpetrator, under *any* of the following circumstances:

— Where a person is incapable, through lunacy or other unsoundness of mind, whether temporary or permanent, of giving legal consent.

— Where it is accomplished against a person's will by means of force or fear of immediate and unlawful bodily injury of the person or another.

— Where a person is prevented from resisting any intoxicating, narcotic or anesthetic substance, administered by or with the privity of the accused.

— Where a person is at the time unconscious of the nature of the act, and this is known to the accused.

— Where a person submits under the belief that the person committing the act is the victim's spouse, and this belief is induced by any artifice, pretense or concealment practiced by the accused, with intent to induce such belief.[3]

Marital Rape

Legally, "marital rape" is a contradiction of terms. Most sexual assault statutes define rape as involving intercourse through force or threat of force, without the consent of the woman, *other than one's wife*. It is this "spousal exemption" which makes marital rape legally non-existent.[4]

As of January 1982, nearly forty states exempt a husband from prosecution for the rape of a wife with whom he is currently living.[5] But between 10 and 14 percent of the married women surveyed in San Francisco and Boston acknowledged a sexual assault by a husband.[6] Hope for the husband and his wife is available. Suggestions for seeking help are found in *Recovery* by Helen Benedict.[7]

There are many who don't acknowledge a husband's enforced sexual advances as rape. Unfortunately, that denial exists even among Christians. Yet if we are honest with ourselves, we must admit that there are sweet, submissive Christian wives who are indeed raped by domineering, authoritarian Christian husbands. God's divine plan for marital intimacy is based on mutual love, respect, and affection. The sexual needs of both husband and wife are to be fulfilled through that love, not through violent sex. Colossians 3:19 says: "Husbands, love your wives." Enforced sex is not love.

Acquaintance Rape

A practice which is increasing on college campuses, and the hardest type of rape for women to report, is "acquaintance rape" or "date rape." According to Maureen Dowd, acquaintance rape accounts for about half of all reported rapes.[8] In this type of assault, the victim knows her assailant. Sometimes she knows him only on a casual basis or in a dating situation. When that's the case, she may fear that people will assume she is guilty in some way; therefore, she will not report the rape. She may also fear retaliation from the rapist. Either way, as Martha Burt, research associate at the Urban Institute in Washington, says, "Women end up being their own worst punishers."[9]

Teenage Rape

According to the Rape Treatment Center in Santa Monica, California, middle school and high school students are especially vulnerable to certain forms of abuse and rape. The center also reports that the sexual victimization of young people is rising at an alarming rate throughout California, especially in the Los Angeles area, which accounts for about 25 percent of all reported cases.[10]

In 60 to 80 percent of teenage rapes, the offender is someone the victim knows, therefore she is especially prone to remain silent, and she doesn't seek help after the trauma. Some symptoms which might be experienced by this silent victim include depression, chronic difficulty in intimate relationships, low self-esteem, and feeling "different" — unable to fit in with others. There is a high risk of developing severe psychiatric disorders. If young people are informed about how to get help, though, many of these problems can be prevented.

Due to the lack of awareness and education about the crime of rape, many programs to enlighten young people are rising up in our communities. A popular three-part TV series, "Better Safe Than Sorry," teaches children three important rules:

1. Say no.
2. Get away.
3. Tell someone.

Hosted by Stephanie Edwards, noted Christian communicator, the programs are geared toward high school audiences and deal with the sensitive and difficult areas of acquaintance rape and sexual pressures among teenagers. This educational tool is being well received in schools and by police departments throughout the country.

Recently a friend sent me a clipping from Josh McDowell's ministry. It told of preparation for launching "Why Wait?" — a project aimed at giving young people solid reasons and ways to say no to sex outside of marriage and effective ways to resist sexual pressures. The basis for this project was a collection of letters presented at a symposium held at Arrowhead Springs, California, in early January of 1986. This symposium on teenage sexuality was attended by twenty-three national denominational leaders representing over 140,000 churches.

Here is a sample from the letters written to Josh McDowell that motivated these Christian leaders to begin the "Why Wait?" project:[11]

> I loved him. He said he loved me, too. But after we did it, he left and called me all sorts of names. The reason I'm writing is, I don't understand it. We went together for months and I thought we had something special. . . I really need help. I have this feeling that no one really cares about me. No matter what I do, I am not able to make any man happy. If it's not too much trouble, could you write back and tell me what to do?

Here is another. This painful story comes from a young Christian in the Southern California area:

> I haven't shared this with anyone, but somehow I think God wants me to share it. Over Christmas I went to Las Vegas to visit my grandma. A date was arranged for me with a boy. We went out and when we got back to my grandma's house, she wasn't there. He then forced me back to the bedroom. He was a lot stronger than I was and forced me down on the bed. Although I said "no-no-no," he pulled off my pants and did what he wanted to with me. I didn't want him to. I had heard you shouldn't dress wrong. I wasn't dressed wrong. I feel so ashamed.

Research has found that kids with low self-esteem are much more easily influenced by peer pressure than those with positive self-images, and are much more likely to give in to sexual pressures because of their longing to be accepted. "Why Wait?" hopes to build up kids' self-esteem and provide their parents with input on how to interact with teens on this important subject.

Through projects like "Better Safe Than Sorry," and "Why Wait?" teens will be better equipped to resist sexual pressure. They will be internally strong enough to avoid compromising situations that could lead to rape.

However, if you are a teenage victim of an unavoidable sexual assault, there are some things you need to know.

What happened wasn't caused by your actions whether you were raped by a stranger or by someone you knew. Although your parents or guardians do not have to be notified for you to receive medical care, you need to let someone you trust know of your trauma. Talking about your feelings will help you feel better. You need emotional support as well as medical care, and most of all you need to know that God cares about what you are feeling. Though it is difficult to understand how or why your sexual assault happened, in Hebrews 13:5 God promises, "I will never desert you, nor will I ever forsake you." You are not alone.

Profile of a Rapist

Bart Devlin writes in *The Sex Offender*, "The man-in-the-street is convinced that the sexual criminal is insane or mentally retarded; that he is brutal, depraved, immoral and oversexed. He is a social isolate who spends his time reading 'dirty' books or haunting 'dirty' movies; a godless, brainless fellow, a 'dirty' old man, crippled or disfigured, dope addicted and incurable." Devlin goes on to say most rapists are a danger to the community *not* because they are compulsive sex fiends, but because they are violent and aggressive.[12]

Menachem Amir, well-known sociologist, did a study in 1971 of 1292 offenders in Philadelphia. He noted that 71 percent of the rapes committed had been premeditated. His studies showed that "the plan to rape was established but the specific victim had not been picked."[13] His studies also showed that in the majority of cases offenders and victims lived in the same area and that neighborhood often was the area in which the victimization took place.[14]

Most experts agree that the majority of sex offenders suffer from personality disorders. One disorder frequently reported is the antisocial or sociopathic personality, meaning having an impulsive lifestyle, and they can be very charming. Their charm, however, is only superficial as they are incapable of forming deep, meaningful relationships.[15] An example of enlisting trust is mass murderer, Ted Bundy, who charmed many of his victims through his mesmerizing manipulations before raping, maiming and murdering them.

The need to dominate and control women to prove their own virility is shared by many offenders. Also, sex offenders often demonstrate low self-esteem, underdeveloped emotions and lack of confidence in their maleness.

Other contributing factors include:
- deprivation
- extreme sibling rivalry
- lack of love from family
- chaotic early environment
- rigid religious instruction
- inadequate sex education
- fear of women that has turned to hate [16]

The potential rapist becomes lost in these struggles and powerless to change the situation in which he finds himself. Nicholas Growth, director of a sex offender program in Connecticut, found that approximately 33 percent of the offenders had themselves been sexually victimized as children.[17]

Mary Cecrle, the sexual assault victim specialist mentioned earlier, talks about three types of rapists: the power rapist, the anger rapist and the sadist rapist.

The *power rapist* uses a minimum amount of force, and his intent is to overpower and degrade. He asks the victim many personal questions and commands her to obey him. He usually does not display a weapon but the ultimate threat of death is always there. He rapes to acquire and maintain mastery or control over someone else. Frequently he is without power in his life, or at least he feels powerless. He usually plans the rapes and carries them out ritualistically, and he gets his satisfaction from the victim's helplessness and submissiveness.

The *anger rapist* is motivated by revenge. Studies show he is furious at someone or something and merely chooses his victims at random. The attack usually is triggered by an insult or an argument with someone else and he wants to punish. He is brutal and begins the attack with violence, often appearing suddenly and jumping the victim.

The *sadist rapist* wants to hurt and does so for sexual stimulation. He usually inflicts trauma on the sex organs and in extreme cases will mutilate or murder. Fewer than 2 percent of rapists fall into this category.[18]

Another study, conducted by the Bridgewater Institute for the Study of Violence in Bridgewater, Massachusetts, reveals four general types of rapists, and concludes that no category is exclusive. This study intends only to give insight into the background of rapists in general, not to define any one personality with accuracy. They are described as follows:

Type: Aggressive-diffusive (aggressive intent); usually impulsive rapes.
Trigger: Possible fight with wife, mother or boss; anger; deflated ego.
Aim: Aggressive acting out; humiliation; mastery and power; pain.

Type: Sexually aggressive-diffusive (sexual intent); usually premeditated rapes.
Trigger: Sexual frustrations; anger; fight with wife, mother or boss; sexual rejection.
Aim: Aggressive acting out; sexual contact; emotional contact; mastery and power; humiliation.

Type: Predatory-aggressive (impulse type).
Trigger: Robbery; anger.
Aim: Aggressive acting out; "ripping off"; mastery and power; some sexual release.

Type: Anal-erotic aggressive (sadistic intent); rapes either by premeditation or impulse.
Trigger: Anger; pain; rejection.
Aim: Aggressive acting out; infliction of pain; production of fear and terror; mastery and power.[19]

What Enables the Rapist to Rape

Writer James Selkin, Ph.D., refers to the man's emotional death which enables him to rape his victims. Selkin writes, "Rape is a scare word. It arouses in women almost as much fear as the word murder, and in a sense it kills both rapist and victim. The offender dies emotionally because he no longer can express or feel tenderness or love, and the victim suffers severe emotional damage."[20]

The rapist's emotional death comes before the rape. The victim's emotional damage comes after. Only through the restoration of her soul by God's love will she be able to conquer the effects of the assault and continue life fully recovered and fully alive. The rapist's soul will have to be left to God and His enactment of justice.

10

Is There Ever an End?

Though easily startled and somewhat fearful — the tendencies left over from my childhood — I believed God's promises. I took seriously what 2 Timothy 1:7 says: "For God has not given us a spirit of timidity, but of power and love and discipline." With His help, I had been working at overcoming my fears and had made progress in becoming friendly and outgoing.

After the rape, I became extremely cautious and suspicious. Since the rape happened the day of spring registration for a night class at Santa Monica City College, I dropped the class fearing the rapist had followed me from the campus that morning when I registered. When in open spaces, waves of panic swept over me and my heart thundered with fright. If the phone rang, I was afraid to answer. Would it be the rapist calling to taunt me? I kept the back door locked and bolted, which frustrated Nicole and Lisa when they arrived home from school and couldn't get in. I was insecure and vulnerable, irritable and moody. Flashbacks, emotional outbursts, depression and self-pity all became regular occurrences in my life.

Will there ever be an end to this nightmare? I'd silently scream, worried that I was going crazy. The plague of phobias wouldn't stop. At the supermarket I was afraid of crowds and afraid to walk to and from my car, and I hated being alone. I remember I couldn't look at a kitchen knife without cringing. If there was screaming on TV, I fled the room and became nearly hysterical, crouching in the bedroom`behind the closed door. Then I would start crying all over again about the horror I'd been through.

If I saw someone with the same type body build as the rapist, I froze. *Is that him? Could that be the man who raped me?* I rarely drove the freeway because I feared the car would break down and I would be stranded, alone, and helpless. Nightmares and violent dreams filled my nights causing me to delay going to sleep. The uncertain future hindered the present. I never knew how I would react in new situations. Frequently I had exaggerated responses to seemingly normal events.

About a year and a half after the rape, I braved an outing to a Saturday matinee with the girls and a few of their friends. While we were there, a fight broke out a few rows ahead of us. I immediately became tense.

"Girls, get your things," I said, my muscles tightening.

"But, Mom, the movie isn't over," Lisa protested.

"Lisa, we are leaving. Get your things *now.* We are getting out of here this minute," I raged.

The girls were embarrassed and irritated about leaving, but I couldn't stay. My brother had been in fights in grammar school and I was terrified then of the violent eruptions of third grade boys. That feeling, now combined with my fears since the rape, sent me into an uncontrollable panic. I wasn't going to wait to see what developed and get stabbed in the process should someone in the theater have a pocket knife or some other weapon. One by one we filed out, tripping over exasperated viewers impatiently craning their necks to see the movie. I was determined to get out of that theater — fast!

We rushed out the entrance and down the sidewalk, the girls muttering all the way. We had to walk through a short alley to get to our car and on the way I noticed a strange looking man coming our way. He was clothed in tattered jeans and an old black leather jacket, and he carried what looked like a stick in his hand. As he passed I became rigid and what I saw was a rapist with a knife instead of a man with an umbrella.

"Mom, what's the matter?" Nicole asked. "You look like you saw a ghost."

"Oh, nothing, honey. Let's just get to the car," I said, starting to half run. "Come on, girls, hurry up."

Once inside the safety of the car, I broke out in a sweat and began trembling. *Oh, God, please help me. I can't go on like this.*

This reaction is common to rape victims, but it is not the only one they experience. There were other times when I became the aggressor. One midweek morning a young man distributing flyers in mailboxes started walking up to our door. Before he knew what had happened I flew out of the front door, arms flailing in every direction, and yelled at him to get away from our house.

"Don't you dare put those in our mailbox. If we wanted them, we'd have asked for them. Get out of here," I screamed at the poor, bewildered fellow. "Don't come back, ever!" I felt assaulted again, and was furious that someone would assume I wanted something when I didn't.

I never knew when this wild behavior would overtake me. I seemed destined to relive the rape constantly through these innocent situations which in my mind were distorted into violations.

One rape victim, Debbie, frequently faced similar feelings of anxiety, triggered by threatening situations that reactivated her past fears. A certain amount of tense time is normal following a rape, but when a victim's lifestyle is constantly interrupted, it's an indication she needs more help. It is necessary at this time for her to talk with a trusted friend, a counselor or pastor. It may also be the time to begin expressing feelings and fears as honestly as possible.

The Healing Process

When I began writing this book, I glossed over much of my internal pain, wanting to communicate victory in Jesus before I'd actually experienced it. Though I deceived myself,

I didn't fool the expert editorial eye of Fritz Ridenour. After reading his review and drying my tears, I accepted his challenge to allow God to heal me from the inside out so I could write firsthand of His power.

That lesson has proven invaluable in my healing process as I humbly admitted my fears and feelings of anger, humiliation and embarrassment at being raped. Another step toward healing involved taking my enormous hurts before the Lord and honestly expressing to Him all that I felt, leaving nothing out.

The right time to begin expressing feelings and fears about her rape will be different for each victim. Some will be ready sooner than others. Ecclesiastes 3:1-4 speaks of the right time for birth and death, and for healing. We can be confident each victim will know when God's time has come for her healing to begin. It may be very private, or it may be open; it may take only a short time, or it may last a very long time. But every road to recovery is like an ascending stairway. Each step the victim takes brings her closer to wholeness and complete healing. Eventually she will be able to comfort other hurting victims.

The following suggestions, based on my experience, may prove helpful to you if you are a rape victim seeking the process of healing.

Allow yourself to cry whenever you need to and wherever you are. Tears bring healing and are often stirred by the Holy Spirit. Let them flow. In God's time, "He shall wipe away every tear" (Revelation 21:4).

Allow your emotions to surface. When they begin to rise up, do not stuff them back down inside where they will stew. God will honor your honest expression — nothing is hidden from His sight anyway. And He is interested in a humble spirit for His service. Isaiah 66:2 says: "I will look to him who is humble and contrite of spirit."

Allow others to give you support. When others are prompted by the Holy Spirit to reach out to you, let them administer the healing balm God has placed upon their hearts.

The rape trauma doesn't end when the rapist leaves — it begins. Healing is like a journey. It is a continuing process.

Sexual Recovery

Many of us are taught from childhood that our bodies, including our "private parts," belong to us. No one is to touch us, look at us, hold us or attempt any invasion on our body. Rape is the ultimate violation and understandably leaves the victim feeling wretched, damaged and worthless.

In Sunday school we learned the body is a creation of God, that it is good and we need not be ashamed of how God made us. But when rape occurs, when the victim's feelings and the value God has placed upon her body are disregarded, shame takes root. She feels ugly and wants to hide. The temptation to devalue herself is all too great. In order for sexual recovery to occur, the assault must be put into perspective and not be allowed to plague the victim for the rest of her life. She will need help and, to a large extent, her recovery will depend on her age, family, marital status and her significant other, i.e., the man in her life.

Children need delicate counsel by sensitive and supportive persons. Teenagers need specialized care — it is crucially important to them that they understand the difference between love expressed sexually and rape as the sexual expression of aggression. In virgin rapes, female support seems most important. It's very helpful if the girl's mother or other close female relative makes herself available.

One fourteen-year-old girl in St. Louis went for a dip in a pool on a hot day in July and was brutally assaulted by two youths who ripped off her shorts and repeatedly raped and sodomized her for forty minutes. Outraged when I read of this in our local newspaper, I was even more appalled that at least three adults stood by and watched as the girl screamed for help. At last, an eleven-year-old boy rode off on his bicycle for help. My anger burst forth in a letter to the editor of our paper, and it was printed. This young girl's sexual recovery will require specialized care if she is ever to have a satisfactory marital relationship. It's vital for her emotional and physical health that her fragile situation be given adequate time and expert attention.

For married victims, the husband's attitude plays a crucial role in her sexual recovery. His view of her after she has been "used sexually" by another man will be felt by the victim whether it's expressed or not. She will sense her husband's doubts if he considers such questions as, Did she enjoy it? Is she sure she was as careful as she could have been? How could she let this happen? or Why didn't she scream and fight? Accusations like these, verbalized or unspoken, will hinder her sexual recovery and be emotionally hurtful to her.

Although the husband or other close male friend will have his own problems, the victim's needs must be met first. The more patient and understanding he is of her needs during this sensitive time, the sooner his own needs will then be met. Her desire for sexual intercourse will likely be lessened at this time, but her need of affection will be just as great if not greater.

Touching, stroking and caressing can help reassure the rape victim she is as valuable and beautiful as before, in spite of the horror she's been through. This will help break down the loneliness and alienation that are waiting to grab at her innermost being. If you are the man in her life, be assured that an arm placed gently about her, a pat on the back, rubbing her shoulders, or a kiss on the cheek communicate her continued worth in your eyes. Most important, you should relate your willingness to let her talk. Because of your closeness to her, she may be more sensitive to your feelings. Should the rape unreasonably distress you, she will sense that and may withhold her feelings. She may also try to protect you by not mentioning details of the rape. In that instance, you may be left with your imagination, fantasizing about what might have happened. This can cause you more torment than knowing the truth.

Resuming Sex

Touching leads to the question of sex. Every rape victim will respond differently about when to resume marital inter- course, and the appropriate time will be different for each individual victim. Some will be ready fairly soon after the rape, using this expression of love as a way to forget. Others will be more hesitant and will need more time. Listening to the victim's comments will help you decide just what her needs are. Also, you can *gently* ask questions to help you determine how to proceed.

To avoid further trauma, which could damage future sexual intimacy, do not press the victim to engage in sexual relations before she is comfortable. Communication and the expression of feelings are vital in the recovery of both the victim and her husband. If, after a reasonable amount of time, she is still struggling with sexual expression, it may be helpful to seek professional counseling.

Some of the problems rape victims may experience in resuming sexual relations with their husbands are:

1. lack of desire;
2. aversion to certain positions or actions; and
3. an inability to have orgasm.

In one study of rape victims, Judith Becker, associate professor at the Columbia College of Physicians and Surgeons, found that continual flashbacks were a most significant factor in the rape victim's reluctance to resume sex. The majority of women in her studies were able to resume normal sexuality within three years, but 39 percent said they were still plagued with problems because of things that reminded them of the rape, even such things as a smell or a certain touch. Those who did not have sexual problems as a result of the rape had these two factors in common: (1) The victim abstained from sex until she was ready for it; and (2) she had a partner who said, "I'm still interested in you; I still desire you. But let's take things at your own pace."[1]

According to Kristi Peek, a licensed marriage, family, and child counselor,

> There is no doubt that many women who have been victims of rape get divorced. However, to determine that the rape caused the divorce would be a difficult if not impossible scientific study. It is common knowledge that the divorce rates have been increasing in recent years for many reasons.
>
> To say that a woman gets divorced because of the rape

would be a suspect conclusion. Entering counseling or psy-therapy *is* very common for rape victims and this could more likely have a direct effect on divorce statistics. While involved in therapy, the rape victim may become aware of dissatisfactions in her life that had not previously been acknowledged. This may include her marital relationship, and unless the husband becomes involved and committed to grow and change with his wife through the therapy process, divorce often results. As the Chinese word for crisis is the same as the word for opportunity, so is a trauma such as rape an opportunity for psychological growth. If the rape victim's husband does not also seize this opportunity to grow emotionally along with his wife, divorce is almost inevitable.[2]

Helen Benedict writes in *Recovery:*

Traumas of any kind shake relationships to their foundations, and if there is already a weakness there, they sometimes exaggerate that weakness to the breaking point. Various studies report a 40-90 percent breakup rate between couples after a rape. No one knows the exact number because many victims are young and in non-permanent relationships anyway.

On the other hand a strong and loving relationship will usually survive rape and help the woman recover faster than any other single factor.

But when sexual or communication problems already exist between a couple, or when there is an imbalance of power, rape will bring these problems out.[3]

She also says, "Learning to trust men again is one of the hardest aspects of recovery."[4] But trusting a known God for an unknown sexual future can lead to healing of emotional wounds and scars caused by rape. God wants to be our source for sexual recovery. Trusting Him will help rape victims trust themselves again and it will lead eventually to the ability to trust in men again.

Value in Christ

Two years after the rape I spent some time talking with Pastor Phelps, the associate pastor of my church at that time.

I hoped he could help me make sense out of my struggle for meaning and purpose, since I had felt robbed of these by the rape. Pastor Phelps explained that as God's child I have worth and value in Christ. Nothing I can do and nothing that happens to me will change that fact. Being raped does not change my significance in Him. Because of that, I can depend on Him to restore my shattered self-esteem.

We have been loved from the beginning and God knows all about us. We can be free in Christ to relax and not strive for significance. In Him, we are significant. We are worthy based on the wealth He alone gave. A rape victim feels anything but worthy, but by focusing on God's wealth, she can experience riches untold.

Steps to Restore Your Self-Esteem

1. Be honest. Be honest with yourself about your feelings. Getting in touch with any unpleasant feelings such as anger or revenge is healthy and therapeutic. Self-validation, recognizing the validity, the authenticity and acceptability, of your own feelings and giving yourself permission to have them, will help restore your self-esteem.
2. Get involved. What interests you? How do you like to spend your time? Is there someone who needs a friend? Helping others is a key to helping ourselves, even if we don't feel capable. God makes us strong in our weakness.
3. Take care of yourself. Your looks, hair color, eye color, attractiveness or lack of it were not the cause of your assault. When you understand that, you can begin caring for yourself again, based on God's Word that declares you are valuable and beautiful in His sight.
4. Read helpful books. *Can You Love Yourself?* is a book on self-esteem written for today's woman by Jo Berry.[5] *Becoming God's Special Woman,* also by Mrs. Berry,[6] will encourage you as you learn to appreciate more fully your value and uniqueness.
5. Believe you are a worthy person. Use a Bible concordance

to locate Scripture verses that speak of your worth. Memorize and believe them. God wants to repair your brokenness and restore your self-esteem, but He needs you to trust and obey by believing His Word.

6. Communicate your needs to your significant other. Some of the things your significant other can do to help in your process of recovery and restored self-esteem are simple and easy. But you will have to communicate your needs. Do not assume that person knows what you need or can interpret your clues.

Communicating your needs doesn't necessarily mean they will be met. It may be your significant other is going through his own emotional torment — he may even feel guilty for not defending you or protecting you from the assault. But no situation is too difficult for God. His understanding is infinite and will encompass both of you during this transitional time of turmoil. If your significant other isn't strong enough to put his own needs aside to meet yours, rest assured God can meet them all for both of you.

Hope Lies Ahead

We can depend confidently on God's restorative power to end our victimization. But for some, release of the problem is necessary. At some point in time the victim must release her sexual assault to God and stop hiding behind the hurts, or she will victimize herself further. She must allow God to heal her from the inside out. When that process is completed and the rape is appropriately integrated into her life, she can end the chronic reactivation of the whole experience.

God's Word instructs us, in Philippians 3:13,14, to press on, forgetting what lies behind. He will give us strength and courage to be faithful servants even after the crisis of rape. Margaret Clarkson writes in *Grace Grows Best in Winter,* "He who is able to bring forth rose from brier is able to make the thorn of your hedge blossom and bring forth fruit. Will you deliberately rejoice in His choice for you, lay hold upon God as your special portion and inheritance, and let Him transform your hedge into a thing of beauty and fruitfulness?"[7]

How to Prevent Rape From Happening to You

D ori continued driving while glancing at her map, trying to find her friend's new house. The recent development on the outskirts of the midwest town was slowly filling with new home owners. Dori wondered if she should stop and ask directions. *Oh, well, I'll just keep going. I know it's around here somewhere.*

As she first turned left, then right, she noticed not only that a dead end was straight ahead, but also that an old, dusty, black Buick was directly at her rear bumper. Forced to stop, her heart jumped as she saw a huge, sloppily-dressed man lunge toward her. He came right up to her car window and she felt an icy chill shoot through her body as he stared at her.

To this day the details of what happened next remain blurred, but Dori tells of pressing hard on the gas pedal and tearing around in a sharp U-turn in a desperate effort to get out of that dead-end street as quickly as possible. She never did know that man's intentions, but when the sudden feelings of fright overwhelmed her, she reacted without waiting to see if they were warranted.

Dori made the right decision by removing herself. We can overcome embarrassing reactions to harmless situations, but waiting to see what develops may prove fatal. One of the first steps toward preventing rape from happening to you is to be aware of the possible danger of your surroundings.

Rape awareness is rape prevention. Three simple points to remember are:

1. Be aware.
2. Be alert.
3. Trust your instincts.

Rape Awareness

Recently I was talking with a woman in her late thirties about rape awareness, and she confided she didn't want to think about it. Her way of prevention was to avoid the whole subject, pretending rape couldn't possibly happen to her. She lived alone and often went home late. After we talked for a while, she finally admitted her fears to me.

Another woman, Vicky, who works at the cleaners I frequent, said she didn't know of anyone who had been raped so she just didn't have anything to do with it. It's false security to believe that if we don't think about it, or that if we don't know anyone who has been raped, we are immune. I believe God holds us as women accountable to become aware in order to arrest the rapid rise in rape.

During an interview of rapists at a prison in Tehachapi, California, it was discovered that not only can a rapist look at a group of women and tell who's been raped, but he can also discern who is prone to become a victim. According to James Selkin, Ph.D., "A potential rapist looks for a woman who is vulnerable to attack. Rapists differ in defining who is vulnerable. Some look for victims who are handicapped or who can't react appropriately or swiftly to the threat of rape. Such a man might prey upon retarded girls, elderly women, sleeping women, or women who are intoxicated. Still other assailants look for environments easily entered and relatively safe." In these cases, the rapist makes sure the victim is alone so he will not be interrupted. Some rapists only attack in the run-down sections of town, where residences are rickety and women live alone. Between 1970 and 1972 in Denver, Colorado, more than three-fourths of the victims were single women.

Dr. Selkin mentions three factors that make women particularly vulnerable to rape:

1. housing that is easy to enter;
2. isolation of the victim;
3. women who are characteristically friendly and who like to help others.

In the Denver study one-fourth of the women victimized by rape had responded to the offender's request for help. Teachers, nurses and other women who have learned to serve others, who are charitable, and who sacrificially give of themselves are especially vulnerable to sexual exploitation, according to Dr. Selkin.

Although we are to be helping and caring individuals, we need to exercise caution and prudence and be sensitive to ploys by potential rapists. One rapist in the Northwest would pull up next to a woman driver at a stoplight. He would tell her she had a flat tire and gallantly offer assistance. Then, after the woman had followed him to an isolated street off the main boulevard and stepped out of her car, he would approach her with a tire iron, threaten her life, and rape her.

Another rapist went from door to door in an apartment complex asking for "Susie." When he found a helpful woman, presumably alone, he would explain how hot and tired he was and ask for a drink of water. After the drink, he would ask to use the bathroom. While there, he would look around to make sure the victim was alone. Upon returning, he would ask for a second drink of water, and as the woman stood at the kitchen sink, he would attack. With a knife at her throat, the woman usually submitted.

Many a rapist, when he finds a woman who appears to be a vulnerable target, will establish some kind of communication with her in order to determine if she can be intimidated. If she can, he then threatens her life. For example, a rapist may approach a potential victim on the street and ask for a light. If she fidgets for a match, he then may ask an intimate question. If she reacts submissively or tearfully, he has found what he's looking for, an intimidated woman who will likely submit to his demands. Intimidation is the name of the game for this rapist.

Other tests they may employ include making suggestive or insinuating remarks, caressing or grabbing the victim, or gauging her reactions by first robbing her. In this way he easily identifies a terrified woman who would submit to rape.[1]

Detective Stephen Manthorne of the Los Angeles Police Department says, "There is something about a victim that attracts suspects." Women must learn not to be so nice, so service-oriented or so helpful. We can fulfill godly living by loving and helping one another, but we also must live responsibly and we must be aware of the methods used by these criminals.

Myths and Realities

So they say, nice girls don't get raped. Nor do business women, dedicated mothers, devoted wives, teachers, college students, adolescents, grandmothers, missionaries or others in Christian service. The truth is, *any* female is vulnerable to sexual assault and can fall victim to this atrocity. The myths surrounding the act of rape are endless. I have chosen ten major ones and listed them below. Following each myth is a statement of fact that will serve to make us aware of reality.

1. MYTH: Sexual assault is committed by a stranger.

    FACT: According to sex crime data, over 80 percent of the victims know the person who sexually assaulted them. The term *know* refers to close friends or relatives, to acquaintances, or to persons whom the victim simply recognizes.

2. MYTH: Sexual assault can't happen if you don't want it to.

    FACT: The victim generally is taken off guard by the perpetrator, thus giving him a great advantage. It's hard for the victim to move fast and think quickly. What works on television is not likely to work in real life, and if an offender has a weapon, it is not wise to resist.

3. MYTH: Sexual assault happens only at night and only in isolated places.

FACT: Sexual assault occurs at all hours, morning and night, and in crowded as well as in barren places. One-third are committed by men forcing their way into the victims' homes.

4. MYTH: Sexual assaults occur in *other* neighborhoods to *other* people.

    FACT: Although some areas are at higher risk than others, sexual assaults occur in rural, urban and suburban areas as well as in metropolitan areas. No geographic area is exempt.

5. MYTH: Sexual assault is something children should not receive information about because it will scare them.

    FACT: Children have as much right to accurate information as do adults. It is more frightening for a child to hear about a dangerous stranger who is going to get them (for what, they are not sure) than it is for them to learn the facts and understand preventive skills and reporting procedures clearly.

6. MYTH: Victims of sex crimes are young, attractive women.

    FACT: (1) Victims can be of any age. Records show some victims to have been under one year and others who were over ninety.

    (2) They may or may not be attractive. An attractive person is no more prone to being sexually assaulted than is anyone else — the crime is not committed because of sexual attraction, but for reasons such as power, fear, anger, low sense of self-worth or early victimization of the assailant.

    (3) Victims are not always female. Male victimization is just beginning to be discovered and reported. In a study of approximately 800 elementary aged students, an equal amount of boys and girls had been victims of some form of sexual exploitation. Many more females, however, were victims of incest and adult rape, which may be due to cultural standards.

7. MYTH: Victims of sex crimes are somehow at fault.

FACT: An offender may think a victim "asked for it" because of how he or she looked or acted. Unfortunately, not only do offenders buy into this myth, but much of the general public does also. Such statements as "She wasn't wearing much"; "She was drinking"; "She was hitch-hiking"; "She did go out with him"; or "Everyone knows what kind of girl she is anyway"; indicate that both men and women often blame the victim, not the offender, for the assault.

Very often victims themselves feel as if the assault was their fault and that they could have prevented it from happening. This self-blame can be extremely damaging and can have long-term effects. Victims need much support and reinforcement to assure them that they are not to blame and most likely could have done nothing to prevent the assault. At times victims may hitch-hike, leave their doors unlocked, be out in a high-risk neighborhood at night, etc.; however, this still does not give anyone permission to sexually assault them.

8. MYTH: A victim probably likes it anyway.

FACT: Rape is romanticized in the movies, on TV, in stories and in fantasies. In reality, though, rape is brutal — far from pleasurable — and it can have long-term traumatic effects.

9. MYTH: Sex offenders are just lonely or sexually deprived.

FACT: Many sex offenders are married or are involved in another sexual relationship at the same time they commit their offense. Loneliness or sexual deprivation may be an underlying factor, but generally is not the sole cause.

10. MYTH: Sex offenders are over eighteen and under forty.

FACT: There is nothing magical about any age. A person does not automatically stop being a sex offender when he reaches forty, nor does he suddenly become one at eighteen. In fact, the biggest population of hidden sex offenders are juveniles. For too long young sex offenders were not identified or prosecuted for two main reasons: (1) the fear that the juvenile would be labeled; and (2) the belief that he would outgrow this type of behavior. Such approaches actually prevented the early intervention necessary to help young people with these problems.[2]

According to Gail Abarbanel, time is apparently the best treatment. As rapists reach their forties they tend to stop.[3] Yet the elderly sex offender must be recognized lest we have a false sense of security because the rapist has passed forty. Statistics reveal that sex offenses have been committed by men who have reached their sixties or early seventies.

Self-Defense

Taking a course in self-defense can be helpful in increasing confidence and in learning techniques to thwart rape. Many women have taken these courses to protect themselves from attack. But let me warn you, for these techniques to be effective you must be proficient in them, and that requires continual practice.

In addition, I strongly affirm God-defense, which is being a responsible Christian through knowing God's Word, claiming it and standing upon it, no matter what. This, combined with your self-defense skills and your increased self-confidence and self-awareness, will allow you to take an active part in preventing a rape from happening to you. It also will give you the means and increase your motivation to work toward general rape prevention rather than saunter passively and naively down the pathway of life, unconcerned.

Submitting to the Attack

If you ever are faced with a life-threatening attack of rape when it's not reasonable to resist (such as when a weapon is being used or children or other family members are threatened), be assured that your submitting out of fear does not imply consent. Rape is rape. It is still a crime even if you do not have a single cut or bruise. As a victim, you should never feel guilty. It is the rapist who has committed the crime.

In the event you are confronted by a rapist, you have less than 60 seconds to assess whether you should take action to resist, get away, or submit. Some experts would say always gouge the eyes or grab the groin, but Frederic Storaska suggests alternatives for action in "How To Say No to a Rapist and Survive."

Here is a list of mental questions to ask yourself:

1. What does this man want from me?
2. What is he prepared to do to me if he doesn't get what he wants?
3. What resources do I have?
4. What defenses can I use against him?
5. Is there anything in the environment that will help me? or hurt me?[4]

You will have to think fast — your life is at stake. Only you know what strategy is best depending on the circumstances. Trust your instincts, then implement your plans. It may even be that during the course of the assault you will abort your initial plan and begin implementing a back-up plan.

Even though every rape situation is different and you will have to do what is right for you, other people's reactions can cause you to doubt the strategy you took. Two years after my rape I still struggled with my submission to the assault. It wasn't until I was a guest on television with the then program director of Defensive Safety Education specializing in the use of tear gas that he assured me my decision saved my life. He told me whenever there is a weapon the prescribed action is non-resistance.

That day I discovered I had acted from a point of strength after assessing — with a knife at my neck — my weakened physical condition and my sleeping child. I had not acted out of stupidity as I had thought earlier.

If your attacker does NOT have a weapon, and depending on the distance he is from you, your physical position (Are you standing, sitting, kneeling, walking, jogging, etc.?), time of day, people around, and whether you see a way of escape, it may not be necessary for you to submit. Run and get away if you can.

Passive Resistance

Sometimes a victim may want to resist but is afraid to scream or fight back. In these cases, a more passive type of resistance may help to "defuse" the violence of the attacker. With passive resistance you can:

Try to calm the attacker. Talk to him and try to persuade him not to carry out the attack. If you win his confidence, you may be able to escape.

Claim to be sick or pregnant. Tell him you have VD [or AIDS]. This may deter the attacker. [But be warned — it also may not. I told my attacker I'd had surgery, hoping he would be repulsed because of the scar. It didn't help.]

Try to discourage the rapist. Some women pretend to faint, some cry hysterically, others act insane or mentally incapacitated. [Although, according to Storaska, if you pretend to faint, you will be even more vulnerable.]

If you're at home, *tell the attacker a boyfriend is coming or that your husband . . . will be home soon.* [However, if you have a roommate and are expecting her to return, do *not* tell that to the rapist. He may rape you, and then rape her when she arrives.][5]

Active Resistance

Nobody can tell you whether active resistance — screaming, struggling, fighting back — will be the "right" thing to do. In some cases, it can frighten off or discourage the attacker. But resistance may also lead the rapist to become more violent or increase his desire to subdue the victim.

There are many kinds of active resistance. Here are some pros and cons regarding the most common ones:

Screaming: A scream can surprise or frighten an attacker away if he fears that people will come to help; but screaming won't help in isolated areas.

Struggling and fighting back: A forceful struggle also may discourage the rapist. If you are not afraid to hurt someone, and can land a strong kick or blow, fighting back may give you the opportunity to escape. *All blows or kicks must be forceful and should be aimed at vulnerable areas.*

Martial arts: Special self-defense courses such as judo or karate are very popular in some areas. . . . [As we said before, skills in these arts can protect you, but those skills must be maintained by constant practice.]

Weapons: Some women carry weapons, such as guns, knives or chemical sprays, to ward off attackers. Unless you are trained and not afraid to use these weapons, *they can be very dangerous.* The attacker might be able to turn them against you. In the state of California, it is illegal to carry some weapons, including all concealed firearms. To legally carry most chemical sprays, you must complete a training course offered by a certified agency or organization. For more information on these courses, contact the Department of Justice Training Center: 916/322-2132. [Every state requires certification for those who carry mace or tear gas, and neither substance can be carried legally on an airplane.] *Check with your local law enforcement authorities before you select a weapon.*[6]

Home Safety

1. List only your initials and last name in the phone book, on mailboxes, door, etc. If you live alone, list another name along with yours.

2. *Think* every time before you leave your name, address or phone number in public view or give out information concerning your daily routine.

3. Use lights by all entrances inside and out and keep your garage well lit. Keep your garage door shut and locked at all times.

4. If you plan to return after dark, leave lights on in various parts of the house. Install timer devices that will activate lights, radio, etc., in different areas of your home and at different times.

5. If you come home and think someone may have been in your home (or still may be inside), do not enter. Go to a neighbor's home and call the police.

6. Do not depend on your dog for more than an alarm if you have a prowler; some prowlers come prepared with poisoned meat or will simply open the gate and let the dog out.

7. If you hear a prowler, turn on all outside lights and call the police. You may want to alert neighbors by phone.

8. Keep your curtains and shades drawn at night.

9. Beware of casual acquaintances who visit unannounced. Many rapists know their victims prior to the rape and plan the time of attack.

10. Ask for identification of all service personnel *before* opening the door. If you have not requested that they make the visit, first validate the office phone number by checking in the directory. Then call their office to verify employment. If you have *any* doubts, do not open the door.

11. *Do not allow small children to open the door.*

12. Do not leave extra keys in obvious places like under doormats, in flower boxes, above the door, etc. Leave them with a neighbor.

13. Do not allow a stranger into the house to use your phone, regardless of the emergency. Offer to make the call for him.

14. When you're home alone, have telegrams and messages slipped under the door and packages left outside. Do not open the door unless you know the person making the delivery.

15. Do not depend on a chain lock on your door. A person of average size can break most chain locks easily. Use a peephole to check on visitors while keeping your door locked. Call through the door if necessary. Also, make sure all doors and door frames are solid and sturdy. Entry doors should be solid-core wood or metal. Good locks, such as deadbolt locks with 1-inch throws, are a must.

16. Lock all windows and doors, even if you go to a neighbor's or make a quick trip to the market.

17. Be aware of places attackers might hide, both inside and outside. Trim bushes and shrubbery, and place gravel under your windows.

18. Do not spend unnecessary time alone in apartment laundry rooms. If at all possible, go in daylight or with someone else.

19. Consider investing in a home security system.

20. If someone is knocking on your door and you're alone, yell out, "I'll get it, Harry."[7]

Awareness in Your Car

1. Check the interior of the car before getting in. Also, look under your car. Some rapists lie in wait to grab your ankle, causing you to fall.

2. Have your car serviced regularly to avoid breakdowns.

3. Keep a CALL POLICE sign in your car to put in the window in case of emergencies.

4. Keep telephone change in your car and tape two dimes to your keys.

5. Keep your gas tank full.

6. If your car runs out of gas or breaks down, raise the hood, quickly get back into the car, and remain inside with the doors locked and windows up. If someone stops to offer help, ask them to call the police or the nearest service station.

7. Have keys in your hand, ready to use, before you start for your car. Fumbling in your purse enroute provides a would-be rapist the opportunity he needs to approach you.

8. Park in well-lighted areas near your destination.

9. Always lock your car when you leave it, even if you're planning to be gone only a short time.

10. Leave a man's tie or pipe on the dashboard to confuse owner identification.

11. Be aware of anyone in the vicinity of your car in a parking lot. If a van has parked next to your car, enter your car from the other side. Vans frequently have become locations for rape.

12. Keep your doors locked and windows rolled up enough to stop a probing hand, especially in stop-and-go traffic. Keep your car in gear at traffic lights.

13. Be familiar with your frequently traveled routes. Know the locations of 24-hour businesses and of the police department and fire stations. Vary your route home.

14. If you discover you're being followed, drive to the nearest police or fire station or open business. Honk your horn repeatedly until you attract attention. Do not drive home.

15. If someone signals from another car that something is wrong with your car, drive to the nearest service station. Do not stop your car to check unless the other car has driven away.

16. Should another car attempt to force you to the side of the road, attempt to keep driving even if it must be through areas not designated for cars. Do not stop your car. If possible, get the other car's license number and drive directly to the police station and report it.

17. Never leave your house keys with your car keys when leaving your car in a parking lot or at a service station.

18. Upon arrival home, keep the headlights on until the garage is opened and the house door is unlocked. If possible, call before going home so a friend or relative can be waiting for you.

19. Do not pick up a hitchhiker, female or male.

20. If you are driving someone home, wait until she has entered the house and signaled for you to leave. Before she leaves your car, establish a code other than waving. If a rapist is waiting inside, he will expect her to wave you on. You might agree ahead of time that she will blink the porch lights to let you know everything is fine but she will wave to you if she wants you to call the police.

21. Arrange for car pools whenever possible.

22. Keep the following essentials in your car at all times: flashlight with new batteries, inflated spare tire, flares, jack, jackhandle, lug wrench, first-aid kit, phone change, paper and pen, jumper cables.[8]

Awareness on the Street

1. Be assertive in your walk, using a firm, steady pace. A passive walk gives an image of vulnerability and sets you up as the easy target the rapist needs.

2. Avoid walking through groups of men. Walk around them on the street side.

3. Plan your route in advance. Walk in well-traveled areas. Avoid bushes, alleys, vacant lots, entryways, and shortcuts through deserted places. Vary your route home.

4. If you think you are being followed, cross the street, change directions, and keep looking behind you so it is obvious you are suspicious, or yell "FIRE!" to attract attention. If you are being followed by someone in a car, memorize the license number and run directly to the nearest business, go inside and call the police.

5. Carry your keys in your hand, between your knuckles, to use as a weapon if necessary.

6. Keep a secure grip on your purse. Do not allow it to dangle. Keep fasteners and zippers on the purse closed and turn the purse so that any openings are close to your body. However, if threatened by a man for your purse, do not choose your purse over your own safety. A purse can be replaced. Money and valuables are safer in an inside pocket of your clothing.

7. Keep your hands free whenever possible so you will be able to resist if someone tries to force you into a car.

8. Carry a whistle wrapped around your wrist or on your key chain.

9. Wear shoes suitable for running. Dress for freedom of movement.

10. If you are waiting outside, stand balanced on both feet. Do not put your hands in your pockets. (Elbows are easy to grab.) Be suspicious of cars that pull up near you or pass you repeatedly.

11. If a driver asks directions, do not get close to the car.

12. Do not walk alone whenever you can avoid it.

13. Do not accept rides from strangers.

14. When using public transportation, sit toward the front of the bus and be aware of every person getting off with you.

15. Never hitchhike.[9]

Awareness of the Telephone

1. List your name in the phone book with initials and last name only, particularly if you live alone.
2. Be wary of telephone surveys. Do not participate.
3. Do not tell people you are or will be alone unless absolutely sure you can trust them.
4. Hang up immediately on obscene calls.
5. If you receive a call that seems to be a wrong number, do not volunteer your number. If the caller requests it, ask him what number he was trying to reach. Then verify to him that he has reached a wrong number, still without giving him your own number.
6. Keep emergency numbers handy.
7. Avoid having young children answering the phone. It may be cute, but it isn't safe.[10]

Going To and From Work

In this instance, apply the rules for car safety. Avoid parking structures if at all possible. If it is not possible, park close to the entrance and remain alert.

On the College Campus

If at all possible, walk with a friend at all times. Be cautious about giving out personal information, even on Christian campuses. If you have a night class, call security to assist you to your car. Park in well-lighted areas.

Babysitting Awareness

Read over the sections on home and telephone awareness. Use caution in telling callers you are the babysitter, alone with the children until such and such a time.

Reality of Rape

In spite of increased awareness, the crisis of rape can strike your life. Although the enemy may cause temporary defeat through taking advantage of a vulnerable moment, God can and will give you eternal victory. But you must seek Him with all of your heart, trust in His promises of healing and restored strength, and believe He will set your feet on higher ground.

> But we have this treasure in earthen vessels, that the surpassing greatness of the power may be of God and not from ourselves; we are afflicted in every way, but not crushed; perplexed, but not despairing; persecuted, but not forsaken; struck down, but not destroyed (2 Corinthians 4:7-9).

I have survived the violent crime of rape. I am a violated woman, yet in Christ, I'm a victorious woman. God is making something beautiful out of my battered life, and He will do the same for you.

12

Once a Victim . . .
Always a Victim?

ello," I answered, one midmorning on a Tuesday.

"Uh . . . hello," I heard a strong, man's voice over the line. "This is Scott. Remember me?"

Scott. Why on earth is Scott calling? Nick isn't here now, he's at work. The nerve. He knew the friendship of many years with Nick had ended some time ago.

"You sound surprised to hear from me," he slurred.

"Well . . . yes, I am. How did you get our number?" I asked.

"I have connections," he said cockily, and then went on to explain how he'd called Phyllis, an old friend, and she had given him our new number.

What! How could she do that? Phyllis had known of the relationship between the two men who were buddies for many years. She also knew they now had gone their separate ways, mutually agreeing to end their bond. And she knew we didn't want Scott to have our number. *Why didn't she call Nick first to let him know of Scott's interest in calling?*

"I just called to see how you guys are doing. How's Nick?"

"He's fine." I said cautiously, again wondering why Scott was calling and what he wanted.

"Is he there?" Scott asked.

"Well . . . no," I hesitated.

"Are you nude?" he continued.

Instantly, I felt as if a boulder had fallen into the pit of my stomach. Thinking I must not have heard correctly, I asked, "Pardon?"

"Are your breasts still small?"

I threw the receiver down, banging it on the phone base! Suddenly hysterical, I began screaming and sobbing. I was terrified. *What if Scott isn't at home like he said, but is at the end of our street? What is on his mind? Why is he doing this to me? Has Phyllis given him our address, too?*

Tears splashed on the kitchen counter as I fumbled with the phone book to call the police. *Stupid me. What are they going to do?*

Almost without thinking I called Phyllis and told her what happened. Her indignant response and lack of empathy added to my distress. *Does she think I am making this up? That being a rape victim makes me unstable, causing me to overreact to an innocent query about the family?*

Although I was angry that Phyllis gave out our number without regard to Nick's feelings, it was evident she didn't agree either that she was in the wrong or that the phone call was obscene, as I indicated. It seemed as though she didn't believe me.

That night when Nick and I talked about what happened, I hoped he would call Scott and tell him just what he thought about the phone call earlier in the day. Nick was shocked, and he was supportive of me, but he didn't feel led to confront Scott. I felt hurt and alone. The crude phone call had reactivated feelings I had when I was raped. I was powerless and helpless once again and felt victimized by the verbal invasions of my dignity. Was I to spend the rest of my life being assaulted by others' lack of respect for mankind?

After a sleepless night, I went before the Lord with my tears, emotional pain and humiliation, seeking what I should do. In the past I'd always looked to others to rescue me and come to my aid. Now, it seemed I was alone and God was calling me to action. He answered that *I* was to call Scott and tell him how I felt about what he had done. He also promised to give me strength to make the call.

After a brief battle with God — which I lost — I found the number and dialed. Scott answered. Fear crept over me. My body shook but my voice was steady.

"Scott, don't you ever do that to me again. If you want to know how Nick is doing, call him at work. But don't ever call here again."

Then I hung up.

Now I was in shock. I had stood up for myself. With the help and empowering of the Holy Spirit, I had courageously spoken up for myself. At first I thought I did it for Scott's sake, but then I realized God enabled and empowered me to do it for my own mental health.

Through that experience God took me another step higher on the stairway to recovery. It was a turning point, and I discovered an untapped strength within me that God wanted to develop further. He had to be sure I was willing to trust and obey.

Chronic Victimization

The mail I've received from women across the nation tells me of lives filled with abuse after abuse. For many it began in childhood with incest or some other form of feeling violated, like not being heard, not being allowed to express feelings, or having the basic needs for love and approval ignored.

Debbie, a woman who was sexually abused in childhood over a period of years at the babysitter's, was raped in her late teens. A pregnancy resulted, and now she is raising her son alone. After reading about rape and incest in *Lives on the Mend* by Florence Littauer, Debbie wrote, "Now I understand why I have let myself go. I have been overweight most of my life and chronically depressed."

Things go well for Debbie until she sees the man that repeatedly molested her in childhood. Then, she resorts to her drinking and drug habits. "I have so much hate toward men that it would be impossible for me to look for a mate," Debbie writes. "My past experience hasn't been too great for me.

They get what they want out of me and then leave me. So, all I have to turn to is the bottle." Debbie is now in counseling and gradually learning to cope. She is a Christian who's been separated from God through many of her trials, but who's considering praying again and being restored to fellowship. Debbie never felt she could reveal her problems at her church. She didn't feel they would understand and has suffered alone through much of her pain.

But Debbie is not alone. She is not responsible for what happened to her, and neither are you if you identify with the mind-set of being a victim. There are things you can do to help stop your victimization.

Self-Image

One way to stop being victimized is by trusting God to restore damaged self-esteem. While the outer trappings of life are the most obvious ways to identify with being a victim, the place to begin recovery is in the inner feelings of low self-esteem. Sometimes intensive counseling — with a commitment to change — is needed to discover the root of this emotionally crippling mind-set.

Bob Phillips, Executive Director of Hume Lake Christian Camps at Hume, California, told me that distorted beginnings developed in childhood can pave the way to chronic victimization and can even lead to a life of promiscuity or prostitution. Even if a child is told she is loved, if she doesn't *feel* loved, she assumes she is not lovable or valuable. Therefore her life experiences are based on a poor self-image. She does not see herself as worthy of kindness, goodness, success, happiness or even financial security. Some women who identify with the victim mind-set live as paupers instead of appropriating the lifestyle of a princess that is available to us in Christ.

It isn't necessary to be a rape or incest victim to be familiar with repeated victimizations. Many women are caught in a web of fear and feel trapped in hopeless situations. Some, allowing others to manipulate and control them, become literal prisoners in their own homes, afraid to venture beyond the supermarket, cleaners or the children's school — if even that far. Given little money by abusive husbands, they are made to feel guilty if they buy a lipstick on sale or want to take a class they are interested in.

One lady told me of a cousin in Texas who had chosen to stay in an unhealthy relationship with her husband rather than risk wholeness, though she constantly was battered physically and bruised emotionally. Another time I received a call from a stressed fifty-eight-year-old woman whose controlling and selfish eighty-one-year-old mother fussed and fumed when her daughter needed the relief of a few hours away from their home.

These women and others like them share the common denominator of low self-esteem. They do not see themselves worthy to be treated with respect and frequently find themselves living life as a doormat. They are members of a society which silently says, "Excuse me for living." Crippled emotionally, they are taken advantage of by family, friends, employers, husbands and children, and they see themselves helpless to change their circumstances.

Power, Love and a Sound Mind

I have had women who are locked in this destructive mind-set tell me they fear they will go crazy. Unvalidated by truths they see, they are tempted to believe what they're told. The old movie, "Gaslight," with Humphrey Bogart and Ingrid Bergman, illustrates this point well. A weakened woman is lying in a psychiatric hospital with her husband at her bedside. Although he has dimmed the lights and she comments, "It's getting darker in here," he denies the room is getting darker. She's convinced she's going crazy, just what he wants her to think.

We read in 2 Timothy 1:7: "For God hath not given us a spirit of fear; but of power, and of love, and of a sound mind" (KJV). Therefore we can believe confidently that we need not live in fear of the future. God will empower us to accomplish positive changes in our lives, and He will restore our crippled minds to sanity.

Passive Versus Assertive Versus Aggressive

The perfect love of God will cast out our fears. He will strengthen us sufficiently for the moments when we need to assert ourselves. We can honestly tell God when we feel afraid, yet trust Him to carry us beyond fear when He leads. Though we are to be in subjection to one another, Christ's death on the cross gave us freedom and we are not to live in slavery or bondage to anyone. Those who try to seduce us into submission will be held accountable, and God will hold us responsible should we fail to speak up for righteousness.

Passive: The passive woman's rights are violated yet she keeps it to herself. Usually she doesn't achieve goals. She feels anxious, unhappy, hurt, defensive, depressed, jealous and frustrated. She is inhibited and withdrawn, allowing others to make choices for her.

Assertive: The assertive person protects her rights while respecting the rights of others. She achieves goals usually without hurting others, has a healthy self-image, and is socially and emotionally expressive. She exudes aliveness and makes her own choices.

She recognizes that a need on someone else's part is not necessarily a call for her to fill it. Accepting these three facts will help you toward healthy assertiveness:

1. You have the right to say no.
2. You have the right to grow emotionally.
3. You have the right to be yourself.

Aggressive: The aggressive person often achieves success by stepping on others. She violates their rights, tends to be defensive, and humiliates and depreciates others. She is explosive, hostile and angry and intrudes on other people's choices.[1]

From VICTIM to VICTOR

When the rape occurred in my life I believed by faith God would work it for my good. I didn't understand how that could be possible but I stood upon His promise. One way God has worked it for my good has been through restructuring, repairing, and replacing unhealthy thoughts and ideas with His truth. Blinded to the truth of my self-worth before my rape, my eyes were opened then and I began to see clearly what had been darkened in the past.

Restructuring: God began restructuring my life first by clearing away the rubble. In the book of Nehemiah the walls of Jerusalem had been broken down by a great battle. The gates had been burned with fire, and before they could be rebuilt, the rubble had to be cleared away. In many ways I was broken down after my physical rape and spiritual crisis. But before God could restore me, the years of rubble and pain had to be cleared away.

Assault by assault, injustice by injustice, violation by violation — from every remembrance going back to my childhood — I went before the Lord and received inner healing. This took place over a period of four days spent at Hume Lake Christian Camp in the Sierra Nevada mountains with Helen Wesel, an inner healing counselor. She led me back into the wilderness of pain and confusion of so many years, but this time Jesus was with me at every turn. Facing my hurts of the past again was very difficult, but as I walked through each one, Jesus held and comforted my aching body, exhausted from tears of travailing.

Repairing: After digging up and clearing away the rubble, God began repairing my brokenness. His healing love began to bind up my mind with emotional health and wellness. Confusion was changed to clarity and I began to see myself complete in Christ.

Replacing: Now, with a repaired mind, I discovered God wanted to replace the negative self-talk I had indulged in with God-talk. Old beliefs were torn down and replaced with His truth. Paul writes: "Therefore if any man is in Christ, he is a new creature; the old things passed away; behold, new things have come" (2 Corinthians 5:17).

Contributing to Change

God promises to do His part and we must do our part. Freedom from chronic victimization requires work. As God leads, we have to contribute by incorporating life changes. Some specific changes to make are emotional, intellectual and physical.

Emotional changes: God instructs us through Paul to mature: "As a result, we are no longer to be children, tossed here and there by waves, and carried about by every wind of doctrine, by the trickery of men, by craftiness in deceitful scheming" (Ephesians 4:14). We are to grow up and be responsible citizens doing what we can to not be victimized.

I began exercising discipline, trusting myself and, finally, accepting myself the way God made me. It was time to risk growing up and becoming the person God created me to be.

Intellectual changes: I needed to read the newspapers, listen to the news and be aware of what was happening in the world. I needed to listen more and talk less. Also, I needed to spend some time in literary classics as well as in God's Word, and allow my mind to be broadened.

Physical changes: A great deterrent to lessening victimization lies in making physical changes. Research has shown that people who stand straight, walk with a firm step, look ahead rather than down, and *act* like they know where they are going, are less likely to be seen as possible victims. When a person's self-esteem is healthy, she reflects confidence and receives more positive responses and less negative ones. Standing tall, sitting erect and speaking clearly communicate strength.

Spiritual changes: This list of four steps will help a woman as she begins to incorporate changes in her spiritual self:
1. Accept the fact that you are fearfully and wonderfully made.
2. Realize that Christ died to give you freedom.
3. Allow His perfect will in your life.
4. Avail yourself of His power and might by which you can be strengthened, can speak the truth in love, and can desire the highest good for others.

How I Stopped Being Victimized

One way God has strengthened me to stop being a victim is through being decisive. Due to a tremendous need of approval, I had become a people-pleaser and allowed myself to be tossed about like a buoy on a deep blue sea. But as I journeyed through the process of recovery and talked with other victims, I noticed many of us had difficulty in making decisions.

Or, once making a decision, we promptly changed our minds for fear it was the wrong one. God showed me through reading His Word and taking a ten-week course called, "Woman Aware and Choosing," taught by Betty Coble, Director of Women's Ministries at First Evangelical Free Church in Fullerton, California, that He wanted me to make decisions. He promised that if I sought wisdom from Him, I could trust Him to help me become decisive. Knowing your own mind and being confident in your ability to think and make wise decisions will help lessen the occurrences of your victimization.

Six Characteristics of a Victim

1. Low self-esteem — how you *feel* about yourself.
2. Low self-image — how you *see* yourself.
3. Self-debasing — putting yourself down through self-criticism and negative self-talk.
4. Helplessness — feeling powerless and trapped in circumstances.
5. Isolation — feeling alone with no support system.
6. Depression — feeling hopeless, believing that no one cares, physically exhausted.

Six Characteristics of a Non-Victim

1. Healthy self-esteem — a sane estimate of self in Christ.
2. Healthy self-image — acceptance of gifts and talents.
3. Positive outlook — self-confident, hopeful.
4. Self-disciplined — in the process of achieving goals.
5. Practicing self-care — treating your body with respect, which includes proper rest, exercise, recreation, social activities and saying *no* when necessary.

6. Spiritually strong — reaching out to minister to the body
    of Christ.

Other ways to aid in not being victimized include knowing
yourself, talking with a mentor or confidante, seeking counseling, admitting you are a victim and asking God to show you
steps He wants you to take. Join a Bible study, trust your
instincts, and search for positives in your own life.

When you take a step of growth up the stairway of
maturity, recognize how difficult it was for you, but realize
that you did it. Picture Jesus at the top of the staircase
extending His arm with His hand outstretched to take hold
of your hand. Believe in yourself. Depend on God to equip
and fortify you. Accept His guidance, His help and His
direction for your life.

If you are victimized by unforgiveness, bitterness, resentment or anger, drop these destructive patterns at the foot of
the cross. Now allow the love of God to replace them with
love, patience and forgiveness of those who have hurt you.
See them as needy people and pray they will see their need
for God to work in their lives.

Self-Examination

Most of us are victimized by the outer circumstances of
life. Yet there are times we knowingly or unknowingly contribute to our own victimization. It's important to allow God to
turn His searchlight into our hearts to illuminate any shadowed
areas. If we really want to walk in freedom as Christ promised,
we must examine our souls honestly. We need to examine our
habits, patterns and innermost thoughts, and we must take
responsibility for our lives. These are some of the obstacles
that can keep you in bondage to victimization:

Unforgiveness: Have you forgiven those who have hurt
or abused you?

Bitterness: Are you harboring a grudge against someone
because something wonderful happened for them and not for
you?

Resentment: Do you resent your spouse, mother, sister,
neighbor, mother-in-law, father-in-law or children?

Anger: Could it be that your state of depression is really anger turned inward?

God does not endorse our going passively or aggressively through life, but He encourages us to assert ourselves when appropriate and to take action. Passively praying in the prayer closet when our two-year-old is standing in the street with a truck fast approaching will not save him from being a victim of a car accident. Going into the street and pulling him to the side will better ensure his safety.

Sometimes God calls us to action and to making changes to reduce our victimization. That is not admitting we are responsible for all or any assaults that come our way. But if there are positive changes you can make toward being responsible and thwarting victimization, God will give you the portion of faith and courage needed to incorporate those necessary steps so you can be set free.

— 13 —————

Where to Go for Help

For nearly three years after my rape I suppressed my true feelings and managed to function. Somehow I'd gotten the idea I was supposed to be stoical, have a stiff upper lip and go on with my life. Almost magically, the mountain before me would be scaled without my actually climbing to the top. What I thought was triumph over tragedy was only a pseudovictory, and it became evident through nightmares, phobias, increased irritability and continued victimization.

Perhaps if the counseling I was receiving at the beginning of the second year had not ended abruptly due to the counselor's pregnancy, my recovery might have been completed without another crisis. Perhaps we all would have been spared a terrifying day. But I must rejoice, because after that the real healing began.

One Saturday morning, as the girls helped me with house cleaning, I became aware of an increasing tenseness. Not understanding the basis for my stress, the more I pretended all was well, the more the tension seemed to heighten. I became a walking time bomb.

Before long, an insignificant situation threw me into a blur of hysteria. Becoming furious with myself at my lack of self control, I lashed out verbally at the girls. I couldn't get ahold of myself, and soon erupted, seething with years of pent-up emotions — some of them going back to my childhood. In a frenzy, I began throwing things. A decorator dish flew across the room, just missing Nicole's head. Next came a TV tray. I didn't care what it hit. Afraid of becoming physically abusive with the children, I slammed the french door that opened to the den. Broken glass shot through the air and then lay shattered on the floor.

"Mommy! Mommy! Please stop! You're scaring us," the girls screamed together.

"Oh, my God," I cried, grabbing my head in unbelief. "What's happening to me?"

Confused and frightened, the girls stood with gaping mouths at their frantic mother.

Devastated by my raging, I slumped to the floor, just inches from the hundreds of tiny jagged pieces of glass. There I sat, tears streaming down my cheeks, sobbing at what seemed to me to be my shattered, broken life.

One at a time, as they realized I was finished with my furor, the girls came over and hugged me between sobs.

That Saturday my barriers were broken and I realized I still was bruised emotionally and needed more help. Humbled and ashamed, I called another counselor. This time I went through my church, and the following Monday I had an appointment with Dr. Stanley Wang, a psychiatrist.

During the next year, a year of intensive counseling, I gradually learned that I had masked my rage about the rape and needed further cleansing, an acknowledgment I had not allowed myself. I, the victim, was becoming a victimizer. I also realized that I was angry at God for allowing this to happen to me. As a Christian I had wrestled with my feelings, denying that I could harbor anything other than forgiveness toward the rapist. I had tried a quiet rebuilding of my life but in that process had discounted my true feelings. Even hidden resentment at Nick for not staying with me on his day off surfaced. Slowly I began to allow myself to feel the hurt, and I finally faced and worked through a number of other issues that had plagued me for many years. I discovered that in many ways my whole life had been a rape. Now, my physical rape was the catalyst that began the catharsis for complete healing and a new life.

A Sign of Courage

There are two types of reaction to rape which come under the heading of rape trauma syndrome, as mentioned in chapter 6. The first reaction is called the *compounded reaction.*[1] The victim experiences not only the symptoms of rape trauma syndrome but also a reactivation of symptoms of previously existing conditions, such as psychiatric illness or unresolved conflict.

The other type is called the *silent reaction,*[2] during which various symptoms occur, but the victim never mentions the rape to her therapist.

The goal of counseling is to return the victim to her previous lifestyle as quickly as possible. She is treated as a woman in crisis needing emergency services. Previous problems are not usually considered a priority when counseling rape victims. But should she have a compounded reaction as I did, additional professional help is often suggested.

Usually the attending physician writes a referral for professional counseling in instructions given to the patient following the initial examination. Victims who have no supportive relationships between counseling appointments are encouraged to make use of available community resources.

Seeking counseling and going to a rape crisis center is a sign of courage and strength, not of weakness. It is not saying that God cannot meet your special needs, but it is recognizing your need of trained guidance in the area of rape and victimization. It is the beginning step toward a smooth recovery, providing the support you need. The support of family and friends is important, but due to the unique psychological needs of victims, professional counseling is imperative.

Results of Neglecting Counseling

Not all victims seek counseling or are willing to talk about their crisis even with a trusted friend. But the damage they do to themselves is greater than any that could have resulted from talking about the rape.

After a television interview on the East Coast in 1985, one lady confided she had suffered silently for thirty years. Another young woman wrote about incest in childhood, two abusive marriages and four children, two out of wedlock. The pain continues for many who do not seek counseling and healing. It may surface in becoming overweight or underweight, or in neuroses, chronic physical ailments, disastrous relationships, broken fellowship with God or even in suicide.

Resources

Part of the aftercare includes a list of names, addresses and phone numbers of community resources for help in meeting medical, legal, and psychosocial needs related to the assault. Resources used as referrals are usually financially and geographically accessible and are capable of responding to the unique crisis needs of rape victims.

In recent years rape crisis centers, rape hot lines, victim compensation programs, victim assistance programs, accompaniment services, emergency room care and specialized training of police departments all have worked together to ensure that if you are or become a rape victim, you do not have to face your ordeal alone. Help is only a phone call away. To avoid further suffering from the serious psychological injury caused by rape, and the emotional stress which may be long-lasting, the following resources are included. They can be a guide for finding help.

To obtain a copy of the National Directory of Rape Prevention and Treatment Resources, write to:

NCPCR
U.S. Department of Health and Human Services
National Institute of Mental Health
5600 Fishers Lane

Rockville, MD 20857
(301) 443-1910

Other Sources of Help

Rape Treatment Center
Santa Monica Hospital Medical Center
1225 Fifteenth Street
Santa Monica, California 90404
(213) 319-4000
Write to request copies of:
Taking Action: What to Do If Raped, and
*Being Safe: Protecting Yourself, Your Family
and Your Home.*

NOVA (National Organization for Victim Assistance)
717 D Street N.W.
Washington, D.C. 20004
(202) 393-6682

ECHOES
P. O. Box 186
Gresham, Oregon 97030
(503) 774-2890 or (503) 658-4821

Church Resources

The following letter to "Miss Manners" was handed to
me by a lady attending one of my "How to Stop Being a
Victim" classes:

Dear Miss Manners:
I am the victim of a violent crime which included rape.
After the event, police formalities, etc., I was in a state of
grief and shock. Although directed to a psychotherapist, I
would have been more appreciative of a display of manners
by those around me. The pastor at my church seemed to feel
my family would be snubbed, even though the armed robber/
rapist had given me no choice. So our pastor forbade me to
speak of the crime to anyone.
Consequently, I found myself unable to explain my grief.
It hurt more to have the pastor offer and ask for prayers for
those who were ill or who had died, but skip our family.

There is no formal color, like mourning, worn by a crime victim, so sudden tears were interpreted as "psychological disturbance."

At the same time, relatives who were informed by my mother sometimes seemed to intrude, asking too many questions. It was just as if they had asked the nature and duration of a disease that had caused death. I didn't want to be reminded of why I grieved. Also, relatives expected me to attend a wedding, and our church expected me to attend as usual.

As being a victim of crime is nothing to feel dignified about, what should I have done?

Among other comments, Miss Manners said in her reply:

It is interesting that you compare this period with mourning. Since formal mourning practices have been abandoned, the bereaved have similar experiences both with insensitive prying and with prodding expectations to behave normally in circumstances for which their feelings are too fragile. . . . You may not be able to get away altogether, but you should certainly eschew ordinary social life until you are recovered. This is the time to draw heavily on the sympathy of your intimates — not the world at large, but those people who are able to set aside time to offer you emotional sustenance in private. And incidentally, your pastor certainly ought to be one of them.[3]
Reprinted by permission of United Feature Syndicate, Inc.

Unfortunately, this type of letter and the feelings communicated by the writer are not uncommon. The church I belonged to at the time of my rape had not established any type of counseling service, nor did I feel the atmosphere was conducive to sharing my crisis. John P. Epp, the pastor in my home town of Visalia, California, who did reach out to me in love and acceptance, was three hundred miles from where the rape occurred, yet his words of comfort and encouragement have remained in my mind and have motivated my recovery. He told me God would use my rape as a stepping stone.

Not every church will be able to have a counseling staff and support network for rape victims. However, every church can have information on record regarding rape hot lines, counseling services and community resources for rape victims, as well as the local victim witness phone number. This information can be available for rape victims who call the church office for help.

Another valuable resource the church can make available is phone numbers of recovered victims who would be willing to offer support to those in need. These women would be excellent sources of love and encouragement because they understand what the victim is feeling. Having been comforted by God, they can in turn comfort another in affliction, thus fulfilling God's exhortation to His people. If churches are not prepared to reach out to rape victims, the body of Christ may lose them to organizations which support views that conflict with Christian beliefs and cause confusion.

Other resources may be found in the yellow pages of the telephone directory under Women's Organizations and Services or Crisis Intervention Service, or in the white pages under Rape Crisis Hotline.

Whether a physical rape is an isolated incident of victimization or part of a lifetime of chronic abuse, if you are a victim, I strongly encourage you to seek help.

Key Source of Strength

Two years before the rape, it was discovered I had a potentially fatal kidney and liver disease. At that time I cried out to God, "Why me? What did I ever do to deserve this?" I finally accepted my physical problems and had turned my focus from searching for answers to accepting my limitations when the rape occurred. "Oh, God, why?" I cried again. "Am I doomed to a life of pain and suffering?"

In the first year after the rape, I focused primarily on trying to make sense out of what had happened. I was consumed with discovering why this horrible nightmare had come into my life, particularly when the pieces of my life's puzzle had just begun to fit together. It seemed someone had bumped the table holding the puzzle. Now, with pieces scattered everywhere, how could my life ever become a picture of order and beauty?

In December of 1984 another discovery was made. My internist sent me to a cardiologist for tests and the results confirmed the suspected diagnosis of a familial heart condition and fluid around my heart.

Once again, I've found it wise to adopt the slogan my husband gave me a few days after the rape. One afternoon I told him I didn't see how I could ever smile again, and he answered, "It's up to you."

Now, nearly ten years later, the choice is still mine. Yes, I must be prudent and not overextend myself, but I can choose to be angry at God and at others for my present physical restrictions, which would likely increase stress and further damage my heart, or I can choose to keep trusting God for strength for the future. I choose the latter. Consequently, I have never felt better or happier. April of 1986 brought a life-changing Caribbean cruise to me, and in August of that same year I hiked up Ten Mile Creek in Kings Canyon National Park near Hume Lake, California.

My special friend, Dr. Sherwood Wirt, once shared with me, "If you believe it's from the Lord, live it to the hilt." The prophet Jeremiah writes in the Old Testament: " 'For I know the plans that I have for you,' declares the LORD, 'plans for welfare and not for calamity to give you a future and a hope'" (Jeremiah 29:11).

It is my firm belief that, had I not trusted Jesus for my life on the afternoon of the rape, I might not be alive today to have a hope or to share my victory. Our God is able to deliver His people from whatever situation threatens to rob your joy. I cannot assure you He will change your circumstances, but I can promise confidently that He will work your pain for good if you choose to trust and obey.

God has demonstrated His faithfulness to me as I've trusted and obeyed. It has not been easy, as you have just read. I once thought that nice girls don't get raped, but I was naive and was living with my head in the sand. Now, according to God, I have a sane estimate of myself with my head in reality.

On the day of the rape, I initially believed I was going to be killed. I *almost* believed there was nothing I could do. But, in a flash, God turned my fears into faith and prompted me to recite Psalm 23. When I said, "Yea, though I walk through the valley of the shadow of death, I will fear no evil: for thou art with me; thy rod and thy staff they comfort me. Thou preparest a table before me in the presence of mine enemies," my fears were relieved. I knew if I died, my God was waiting for me and I would dwell in His house forever. *You can do anything to me you want,* I remember thinking, *but you can't take my Jesus from me. I willingly surrender my soul for God's will in my life.* For some reason, God saw fit to spare my life that day, and He continues to demonstrate His faithfulness through my new life in Christ.

My dear friend, I do not know your specific need or the burden upon your heart. But my faithful friend Jesus does. In whatever state you find yourself, I love you. Whether you are the victim, the mother, the father, the sister, the brother, the friend, the pastor, the counselor or the rapist, our God reigns. I'm praying for you, that you too will trust His redeeming love to transform your pain into eternal gain.

> Then I will make up to you for the years that the swarming locust has eaten, the creeping locust, the stripping locust, and the gnawing locust, my great army which I sent among you. And you shall have plenty to eat and be satisfied, and praise the name of the LORD your God, who has dealt wondrously with you; when my people will never be put to shame" (Joel 2:25,26).

The following poem by Helen Steiner Rice expresses God's desire that we use our own hurts and the comfort we have received to help heal the wounds of others:

HEALING THE WOUNDS OF OTHERS

> Let me not live a life that's free
> From the things that draw me close to Thee,
> For how can I ever hope to heal
> The wounds of others I do not feel —
> If my eyes are dry and I never weep,
> How do I know when the hurt is deep,
> If my heart is cold and it never bleeds,
> How can I tell what my brother needs,

For when ears are deaf to the beggar's pleas,
And we close our eyes and refuse to see,
And we steel our hearts and harden our mind,
And we count it a weakness whenever we're kind,
We are no longer following the Father's way,
Or seeking His guidance from day to day —
For without crosses to carry and burdens to bear,
We dance through a life that is frothy and fair,
And "chasing the rainbow" we have no desire
For roads that are rough and realms that are higher —
So spare me no heartache or sorrow, dear Lord,
For the heart that is hurt reaps the richest reward,
And God enters the heart that is broken in sorrow
As He opens the door to a brighter tomorrow,
For only through tears can we recognize
The suffering that lies in another's eyes.[4]

Exercises for Use in Individual or Group Study

Chapter 1

Review my experience of reciting memorized Scripture during the rape. Read Psalm 41:1,2. Discuss it (if in a group situation) and apply it to your personal situation.

Chapter 2

Review the moments when I saw my ashen reflection in the mirror. Read 2 Corinthians 4:8,9 and apply to your situation.

Chapter 3

Review the time when the Lord gave direction in what to do next and how Carol had been prepared. Read Psalm 32:8 and apply to your situation.

Chapter 4

Review the medical examination and consider the courage required to get through it. Think about the source of greatest comfort and discuss how to appropriate that comfort. If you have not yet accepted Jesus Christ as your Savior, consider this your opportunity to do that. Read John 3:16; Romans 3:23;

Romans 5:8; and Revelation 3:20; and apply them to your situation. You may want to seek help in doing this.

Chapter 5

Notice how each person I encountered was hand-picked by God to meet my needs of the moment: the nurse mentioned in the previous chapter, the two policemen in this chapter, and my support person. Read Psalm 103:11 and Psalm 107:1 and apply them to your situation.

Chapter 6

Review my inner battles with revealing my experience, especially when the Holy Spirit prompted me to tell Joe about it. Read Proverbs 14:18 and Proverbs 12:18. Apply these verses to your situation.

Chapter 7

Review my feeling that nice girls don't get raped, and apply to your situation. Read Genesis 50:20 and name at least two ways you have seen good come from your rape or from that of a victim you know.

Chapter 8

Review my sense of deep depression at feeling abandoned by God. Read Psalm 136:16 and acknowledge where you are in your journey through the wilderness. Also read Mark 11:25

and discuss the decision to forgive and how it applies to your situation.

Chapter 9

Examine the view you historically have had of rape and examine how your view may have changed as you have learned more about it. Consider the rapist's need as you read Ephesians 2:1-6. Read also Psalm 37:7 and apply it to your situation.

Chapter 10

Note the recurrences of my agoraphobia and nightmares. Consider how you can allow yourself time to grieve and to express your mourning through verbal and/or emotional release. Read Isaiah 41:10 and Psalm 91:4,5 and apply them to your situation.

Chapter 11

Review the different ploys used by rapists. Open your mind to God's wisdom and mentally commit to becoming aware, alert and trusting of your God-given instincts. Read Ephesians 6:11,12 and apply to your situation.

Chapter 12

Review my change of behavior in verbal assertion toward Scott. Read Psalm 18:47,48 and Psalm 46:1 and apply them to your situation.

Chapter 13

Review the violent emotional outburst resulting from years of suppressed anger. Read Psalm 37:23,24 and Psalm 119:30-32 and 49-56. Apply to your journey of emotional healing.

ADDITIONAL BIBLE READING AS A BASIS FOR PRAYER AND STUDY

1. Isaiah 26:3 (KJV): Thou wilt keep him in perfect peace, whose mind is stayed on thee: because he trusteth in thee.
2. Proverbs 3:5,6 (KJV): Trust in the LORD with all thine heart; and lean not unto thine own understanding. In all thy ways acknowledge him, and he shall direct thy paths.
3. 2 Corinthians 4:7-9 (NASB): But we have this treasure in earthen vessels, that the surpassing greatness of the power may be of God and not from ourselves; we are afflicted in every way, but not crushed; perplexed, but not despairing; persecuted, but not forsaken; struck down, but not destroyed.
4. 1 Thessalonians 5:16-18 (NASB): Rejoice always; pray without ceasing; in everything give thanks; for this is God's will for you in Christ Jesus.

NOTES

Chapter 2
1. *Sexual Assault Prevention Training Guide* (Sacramento, CA: Crime Prevention Center, September 1981), p.5.
2. Maureen Dowd, "Rape: The Sexual Weapon," *Time* (September 5, 1983), p. 28.
3. David Viscott, M.D., *The Language of Feelings* (New York: Pocket Books, 1976), p. 53.

Chapter 3
1. Shirley Gardiner and Janet Torge, *A Book About Sexual Assault* (Montreal: Montreal Health Press, 1979), p. 32.

Chapter 4
1. Shirley Gardiner and Janet Torge, *A Book About Sexual Assault* (Montreal: Montreal Health Press, 1979), p. 31.
2. "What the Exam Will be Like," *Survivor* (Los Angeles: Los Angeles Commission on Assaults Against Women, 1983), p. 2.
3. See Janet Rosecrans, M.A., ed., *Rape Awareness Handbook* (Cypress, La Palma, Los Alamitos, CA: Police Departments), p. 22.
4. From a telephone interview with the Birth Control Institute Doctors Offices, 1815 W. Ave. Suite E, Fullerton, CA 92633.
5. Rosecrans, *Handbook,* p. 24.
6. Ethel Waters, *To Me It's Wonderful* (New York: Harper & Row, 1972), p. 45.

Chapter 5
1. From rape fact sheet compiled by Gail Abarbanel, L.C.S.W., and Stephen P. Klein, Ph.D. (distributed by Rape Treatment Center, Santa Monica Hospital Medical Center, 1225 Fifteenth Street, Santa Monica, CA 90404, ©1981).
2. *Survivor* (Los Angeles: Los Angeles Commission on Assaults Against Women, 1981), p. 7.
3. Maureen Dowd, "Rape: The Sexual Weapon," *Time* (September 5, 1983), p. 28.

4. "Victim Resistance Standard," *NASW* (National Association of Social Workers) *Newsletter* (March 1981), 26:3.
5. *Los Angeles Times* (August 25, 1985), Metro section, p. 1.
6. *Survivor,* p. 8.

Chapter 6

1. Ord L. Morrow, "Victors, Not Victims!" *Good News Broadcaster* (November 1978), p. 4.
2. Quoted from the book, *If She Is Raped: A Book for Husbands, Fathers, and Male Friends* by Alan McEvoy and Jeff Brookings (Holmes Beach, FL: Learning Publications, 1984), p. 82.
3. Ibid.
4. See Flora Colao and Tamar Hosansky, *Your Children Should Know* (Indianapolis: Bobs-Merrill, 1983).

Chapter 7

1. Shirley Gardiner and Janet Torge, *A Book About Sexual Assault* (Montreal: Montreal Health Press, 1979), p. 5.
2. Maureen Dowd, "Rape: The Sexual Weapon," *Time* (September 5, 1983), p. 27.
3. *Survivor* (Los Angeles: Los Angeles Commission on Assaults Against Women, 1981), p. 9.
4. Dr. Nicholas Growth, "Men Who Rape: The Psychology of the Offender," *Time* (September 5, 1983), p. 27.
5. Janet E. Rosecrans, M.S., ed., *Rape Awareness Handbook* (Cypress, La Palma, Los Alamitos, CA: Police Departments), p. 4.
6. Ibid., p. 5.
7. Ibid.
8. Ibid., pp. 5-6.
9. *Survivor,* p. 10.

Chapter 8

1. Marie M. Fortune, *Sexual Violence: The Unmentionable Sin* (New York: Pilgrims Press, 1983), p. 158.
2. Lewis B. Smedes, *Forgive and Forget* (New York: Simon & Schuster, 1984), p. 47.
3. R. J. Smyth, "Torn by Tragedy — Repaired by Jesus Christ," *Seek* (April 27, 1986), p. 4.

Chapter 9

1. Bart Devlin, *The Sex Offender* (Boston: Beacon Press, 1978), p. 6.
2. Helen Benedict, *Recovery* (Garden City, NY: Doubleday, 1985), p. 1.
3. *Sexual Assault Prevention Handbook* (Sacramento, CA: Crime Prevention Center, 1982), p. 4.
4. Ann Wolbert Burgess, ed., *Rape and Sexual Assault: A Research Handbook* (New York and London: Garland Publishing, 1985), p. 146.
5. Ibid., p. 156.
6. Ibid., p. 148.
7. Benedict, *Recovery,* p. 139.
8. Maureen Dowd, "Rape: The Sexual Weapon," *Time* (September 5, 1983), p. 28.
9. Ibid.
10. See *Child Sexual Abuse Prevention: School-Based Programs for Students, School Personnel, and Parents* (distributed by the Rape Treatment Center, Santa Monica Hospital Medical Center, 1225 Fifteenth St., Santa Monica, CA 90404).
11. Letters to Josh McDowell used by permission of Josh McDowell Ministry, "Why Wait?" Box 1000, Dallas, TX 75221.
12. Devlin, *Offender,* pp. 1,5.
13. Benedict, *Recovery,* p. 6.
14. Devlin, *Offender,* p. 5.
15. Ibid., p. 12.
16. Ibid., pp. 33-34.
17. Dr. Nicholas Growth, "Men Who Rape: The Psychology of the Offender," *Time* (September 5, 1983).
18. Mary Cercle, quoted by Rod Speer in "Talking Can Speed Rape Victims' Recovery," *The Register* (Santa Ana) (October 10, 1984), Metro Section, p. 2.
19. Quoted by Janet E. Rosecrans, M.A., ed., in *Rape Awareness Handbook* (Cypress, La Palma, Los Alamitos, CA: Police Departments), pp. 8-10.
20. James Selkin, "The Mind of the Rapist," *Advisor* (reprinted from *Psychology Today,* January 1975), p. 58.

Chapter 10

1. Judith Becker, quoted by Helen Benedict in *Recovery* (Garden City, NY: Doubleday, 1985), p. 38.
2. Kristi Peek, M.S., Licensed Marriage, Family, Child Counselor, Friendly Hills Medical Group, 951 South Beach Blvd., La Habra, CA 90631.
3. Benedict, *Recovery,* p. 107.
4. Ibid., pp. 39-40.
5. Jo Berry, *Can You Love Yourself?* (Ventura, CA: Regal, 1978).
6. Jo Berry, *Becoming God's Special Woman* (Westwood, NJ: Fleming H. Revell, 1968).
7. Margaret Clarkson, *Grace Grows Best in Winter* (Grand Rapids: Eerdmans, 1984), p. 81.

Chapter 11

1. From James Selkin, "The Mind of the Rapist," *Health Advisor* (reprinted from *Psychology Today,* January 1975), pp. 58-60.
2. *Rape Myths and Realities* (distributed by Sexual Assault Service Community Crisis Center, 4910 Auburn Avenue, Bethesda, MD 20814).
3. From rape fact sheet compiled by Gail Abarbanel, L.C.S.W., and Stephen P. Klein, Ph.D. (distributed by Rape Treatment Center, Santa Monica Hospital Medical Center, 1225 Fifteenth Street, Santa Monica, CA 90404, ©1981).
4. Based on Frederic Storaska, *How to Say No to a Rapist and Survive* (New York: Random House, 1975), p. 71.
5. *Sexual Assault Prevention Handbook* (distributed by Crime Prevention Center, Office of the Attorney General, 555 Capitol Mall, Suite 290, Sacramento, CA 95814), p. 8.
6. Ibid.
7. Based on the *Rape Awareness Handbook,* prepared by Janet E. Rosecrans, M.A. (Cypress, La Palma, Los Alamitos, CA: Police Departments).
8. Ibid.
9. Ibid.
10. Ibid.

Chapter 13

1. Based on information sheet on rape trauma syndrome (distributed by the Santa Monica Rape Treatment Center, Santa Monica Hospital Medical Center, 1225 Fifteenth Street, Santa Monica, CA 90404).
2. Ibid.
3. *Orange County Register* (California) (January 13, 1986), Accent section.
4. Fred Bauer, *The Priceless Gift: The Poems of Helen Steiner Rice, A Fond Recollection* (Princeton: Littlebrook Publishing, 1984), p. 95.